Kansas City CUISINE

Kansas City CUISINE

A Sampling of Restaurants & Their Recipes

Compiled and Edited by

SHIFRA STEIN & KAREN ADLER

Two Lane Press

ISBN 1-878686-18-6

Printed in the United States of America

Cover design, hand lettering, and text ornaments: Calvert Guthrie
Editing and text design: Jane Doyle Guthrie

Two Lane Press
4245 Walnut Street
Kansas City, Missouri 64111
(816) 531-3119

First printing, October 1990
Second printing, 1991
Third printing, 1993
Fourth printing, 1994
Fifth printing, 1995
Sixth printing, 1996

To Bob Barrett, Jason Stein, and Dick Adler,
for their understanding, support, and love.

▓ Contents

◼ Acknowledgments

We gratefully acknowledge the many fine Kansas City restaurateurs
who contributed such excellent recipes to our book. We also wish to thank
Cal Guthrie, Jane Guthrie, Paul Kirk, Bob Barrett, Carolyn Wells, Mary
Spitcaufsky, Jill Adler, Karen Nash, Bonnie Hudson, Ed Laird, Rick Anderson,
Matt Connolly, and Mary Raizman for their invaluable help and advice.

▧ Introduction

Kansas City's long-held reputation as a meat and potatoes town has undergone a major change in recent years. While its steaks are impeccable and its barbecue reknowned, Kansas City's recent development of eclectic and cross-cultural cuisine offers a wide selection of dining experiences. From cafes and tucked-away bistros to traditional steak houses and upscale restaurants, *Kansas City Cuisine* captures a melting pot of styles—French, Italian, Greek, Mediterranean, Continental, Argentinian, Southwestern, Nouvelle American, and just plain "down home."

Our chefs, keeping abreast of national trends, are meeting health-conscious demands by devising innovative dishes that feature fresh produce, lean meats, vegetable and fruit sauces and salsas, and unusual ingredients, merging the exotic with the robust flavors of the Heartland.

Of the 100 or so restaurants we invited to contribute, almost half responded, providing our readers with favorite house specialties as well as some "off-the-beaten menu" creations. An overwhelming number of appetizers and entrées feature poultry, pasta, fish, game, and veal, but we didn't forget our Kansas City roots—you'll find several basic as well as out-of-the-ordinary beef and pork recipes that will dazzle the taste buds.

All of our participating chefs and restaurant owners have adapted their recipes for home use. Most of the dishes rely on easily accessible ingredients, but a few include items that may be available only in gourmet or specialty stores. Be adventurous!

Now you can enjoy the culinary talents of our area chefs without ever leaving home. All that's needed is a sense of your own taste and style, and, of course, the delightful collection of recipes found in *Kansas City Cuisine*.

Shifra Stein
Karen Adler

Beginnings

❦ Mixed Green Salad

2 cups romaine lettuce
2 cups Bibb lettuce
2 cups spinach
4 tablespoons olive oil
1 lemon, zest and juice
1/3 cup feta cheese
2 cups strawberries, each cut
 into quarters

Wash greens, remove stems, and tear into bite-sized pieces. Place in a large mixing bowl. Combine olive oil, lemon zest, and lemon juice, and toss with greens until all leaves are evenly coated. Arrange on serving plates. Sprinkle with feta cheese and garnish with strawberries.

Serves 4 to 6

FITZPATRICK'S

❧ Shredded Romaine Salad

1 head romaine lettuce
1 cup radishes
1/4 cup olive oil
Juice of 1 lime
2 teaspoons sugar
1 teaspoon minced garlic
1 tablespoooon Dijon mustard
1 tablespoon Worcestershire
  sauce
Salt and white pepper to taste
Tabasco to taste

Wash, dry, and thinly slice lettuce and radishes. Combine remaining ingredients and blend well. Lightly toss lettuce and radishes in dressing. Serve very chilled. (*Note:* Dressing keeps 5 to 6 days refrigerated.)

Serves 6

ANDE-LEI'S CAFE

❦ Beefsteak Tomato and Fresh Mozzarella Salad with Tarragon Vinaigrette

8 (3/4-inch) slices ripe tomato, cut in half
8 (2-ounce) slices fresh mozzarella cheese, cut into triangles
4 tablespoons chopped fresh oregano
12 leaves fresh basil

On four 9-inch round salad plates, alternate tomato and mozzarella slices. Ladle 1/4 cup of **Tarragon Vinaigrette** over the slices. Sprinkle top of each salad with chopped oregano and garnish center with 3 fresh basil leaves. (*Note:* Save any leftover vinaigrette in a tightly closed jar and chill for later use.)

Serves 4

Tarragon Vinaigrette

1-1/2 cups olive oil
1/3 cup tarragon vinegar
2 tablespoons Dijon mustard
1 teaspoon dry oregano
1/2 teaspoon dry basil
1/2 teaspoon salt
1/4 teaspoon white pepper

Mix together all ingredients and chill until ready to use.

Makes about 2 cups

FIGLIO
209 West 46th Terrace
Kansas City, Missouri 64112
(816) 561–0505

❦ Caesar Salad Savoy

1 head romaine lettuce
1 large clove garlic
2 anchovy filets
1/8 teaspoon salt
1/2 teaspoon fresh ground
   black pepper
Juice of 1/2 large lemon
1 teaspoon red wine vinegar
3 tablespoons extra virgin olive
   oil
1 tablespoon Worcestershire
   sauce
1 medium egg, boiled for 60
   seconds
1/2 cup Parmesan cheese
1 cup plain croutons

Wash lettuce well. Dry leaves with a towel and chop coarsely. Set aside. Using a fork, mash garlic and anchovies in a large wooden bowl until well blended. Add salt and pepper. Using a wooden spoon, continue mashing mixture until completely spread on the inner bowl surface.

Add lemon juice, vinegar, olive oil, and Worcestershire sauce. Using the back of the spoon again, spread over inside of bowl for 2 minutes or until well blended. Add boiled egg to mixture and whisk rapidly with a fork until mixture is soupy. Add lettuce and toss until leaves are evenly coated with mixture. Add half of Parmesan cheese and toss. Add croutons and balance of Parmesan cheese and toss until well mixed. Serve on cold plates.

Serves 2 to 3

SAVOY GRILL
9th and Central Streets
Kansas City, Missouri 64105
(816) 842–3890

❧ Chilled Pork Salad with Cranberry-Walnut Vinaigrette

2 pounds boneless pork loin, trimmed of fat
Salt, pepper, and garlic powder to taste
1-1/2 cups peeled, seeded, and cubed papaya
1-1/2 cups peeled and sliced orange
1-1/2 cups cored and cubed Red Delicious apple
1 cup toasted walnut pieces
6 large lettuce leaves, washed and dried
1 kiwi, peeled and sliced
6 large strawberries

Season meat in roasting pan and bake at 325 degrees until meat thermometer reads 165 degrees (about 40 minutes). Cool and refrigerate.

Toss papaya, orange, apple, and walnuts in **Cranberry-Walnut Vinaigrette** to make a fruit salad. Place a lettuce leaf over half of each plate. Spoon about 1 cup fruit salad onto lettuce. Thinly slice chilled pork loin and fan 3–4 slices over opposite side of plate. Ladle 1/3 cup vinaigrette over top of meat on each plate. Garnish with kiwi slices and a strawberry.

Serves 6

Cranberry-Walnut Vinaigrette

2 whole eggs, room temperature
2 teaspoons salt
1 teaspoon white pepper
1/2 teaspoon garlic powder
1/4 cup sugar
1/2 teaspoon dry mustard
1 cup fresh cranberries, pureed
2 cups salad oil
1/2 cup red wine vinegar
1/2 cup toasted walnut pieces

In mixing bowl, whip eggs until light and fluffy. Add dry ingredients and berries. Whip to blend thoroughly. Slowly whip in salad oil, blend in vinegar, and add walnuts last. Refrigerate until thoroughly chilled.

Makes about 3 cups

RAPHAEL RESTAURANT
The Raphael Hotel, 325 Ward Parkway
Kansas City, Missouri 64112
(816) 756–3800

❧ Romaine Salad with Garlic Parmesan Dressing and Polenta Croutons

2 heads red romaine lettuce,
  washed, ribs removed, and
  torn
2 heads green romaine lettuce,
  washed, ribs removed, and
  torn
1/2 cup shaved imported
  Parmesan cheese

Keep greens chilled in refrigerator until ready to use. Prepare **Polenta Croutons**.

Remove lettuce from refrigerator and toss with 1-1/2 cups **Garlic Parmesan Dressing** and half the Parmesan cheese. Place the greens on 8 plates and top with remaining Parmesan cheese and hot croutons.

Serves 8 to 10

Polenta Croutons

2-3/4 cups water
1-1/2 teaspoons salt
1-1/4 cup yellow cornmeal
6 cups peanut oil

In a 4-quart saucepan, bring salt and water to a rolling boil. Add 1 cup cornmeal, stirring constantly to avoid lumps. Cook until mixture pulls from the sides of the pan and forms a ball. Press mixture into a 9-inch pan lined with plastic wrap. Place in refrigerator, uncovered, to cool. Remove from pan and dice into 1/2-inch by 1/2-inch croutons.

Place peanut oil in a 4-quart sauce pan and heat oil to 350 degrees. Dredge croutons in remaining cornmeal. Fry the croutons in hot oil until crisp. Remove from oil with a slotted spoon and drain on paper towels.

Garlic Parmesan Dressing

1/2 cup Dijon mustard
1 tablespoon garlic, roasted
8 anchovy fillets
1 tablespoon balsamic vinegar
7 tablespoons lemon juice
1 shallot, peeled
3 egg yolks
1 cup extra virgin olive oil
2 cups vegetable oil
Salt and white pepper to taste

Place the first 7 ingredients in a blender. Blend until smooth. Add the oils in a slow drizzle, incorporating thoroughly. Season with salt and pepper.

Makes 4 cups

MILANO
2450 Grand Avenue, Crown Center
Kansas City, Missouri 64108
(816) 426–1130

❧ Springtime Lamb Salad with Walnut Vinaigrette

3 pounds lamb loin, boned and
  trimmed
3 cups dry red wine
1 cup chopped carrots
1 cup chopped yellow onion
3/4 cup white vinegar
1/2 cup chopped celery
3 sprigs fresh rosemary
4 tablespoons fresh thyme
3 cloves garlic, peeled
1 tablespoon juniper berries
Salt and freshly ground black
  pepper to taste
4 tablespoons oil
1 head red lettuce
1 head leafy green lettuce
4 tomatoes
4 avocados
2 red bell peppers, roasted
2 green bell peppers, roasted
1 pound green beans, blanched
3 tablespoons snipped chives

Prepare a marinade by combining wine, carrots, onions, vinegar, celery, rosemary, thyme, garlic, and juniper berries. Marinate lamb in this mixture, covered and refrigerated, for 24 hours, turning twice.

Drain meat, pat dry, and season well with salt and pepper. Heat oil in skillet and quickly sear lamb. Roast lamb in oven at 350 degrees for approximately 20 minutes until medium rare. Remove from oven and set aside for 15 minutes in a warm place.

Wash and dry lettuce greens. Peel, seed, and julienne the tomatoes, avocados, and peppers. To assemble salads, arrange lettuce, green beans, tomatoes, avocados, and peppers attractively on plates. Slice the lamb 1/8-inch thick and place in the center of salads. Drizzle with **Walnut Vinaigrette**. Sprinkle with chives and serve immediately. (*Note:* This dish must be served right away—the hot items on the cold salad will make the lettuce wilt.)

Fresh garlic melba toast makes a nice accompaniment to this lovely salad.

Serves 8

Walnut Vinaigrette

1/2 cup sherry vinegar
2 tablespoons lemon juice
2 tablespoons Dijon mustard
2 tablespoons finely chopped
    shallots
3 cloves garlic, minced
1-1/3 cup walnut oil
Salt and freshly ground black
    pepper to taste

Combine vinegar, lemon juice, mustard, shallots, and garlic. Slowly whisk in walnut oil and season with salt and pepper. (*Note:* Vinaigrette may be prepared 1 or 2 days in advance to enhance the flavor. Serve at room temperature.)

Makes about 2 cups

THE BRASSERIE BAR & CAFE
Westin Crown Center Hotel, One Pershing Road
Kansas City, Missouri 64108
(816) 391-4472

❧ Marty's Bar-B-Q House Dressing

2 cups Marty's Bar-B-Q Sauce
   (available in area stores or at
   the restaurant)
1 cup Italian dressing

Shake ingredients in a quart jar until mixed thoroughly. Serve over any green or combination salad. (*Note:* Dressing may be used immediately after mixing and stored in refrigerator up to 1 month.)

This dressing makes a good marinade or baste for any meat, fish, or poultry dish. For a sweeter variation, add sugar to taste (approximately 1/2–1 teaspoon).

Makes 3 cups

MARTY'S BAR-B-Q
2516 N.E. Vivion Road
Kansas City, Missouri 64118
(816) 453–2222

❧ R.C.'s Vinegar and Oil Salad Dressing

1 (10-ounce) can Campbell's
   tomato soup
10 ounces vegetable oil
15 ounces white vinegar
2–3 tablespoons salt
1/2 scant cup sugar
2-1/2 tablespoons chopped
   onion
2 tablespoons minced garlic
3/4 teaspoon Worcestershire
   sauce

Combine ingredients and stir well. (*Note:* This can be made up to a week in advance and stored at room temperature or refrigerated.)

This dressing also can be used as a marinade.

Makes about 5 cups

R.C.'S RESTAURANT
330 East 135th Street
Kansas City, Missouri 64145
(816) 942–4999

❧ Stephenson's Potato Soup

8 medium (6-ounce) potatoes,
   peeled and diced
3 tablespoons butter
1 medium carrot, chopped
1/2 cup finely chopped onion
3 tablespoons flour
6 cups milk
2 tablespoons finely chopped
   fresh parsley
2–4 teaspoons salt
3/4 teaspoon seasoned salt
1/3 teaspoon MSG (optional)
1/3 teaspoon red pepper
1-1/2 teaspoons granulated
   chicken boullion

Cook diced potatoes in boiling, salted water. Drain and set aside. Melt butter in a separate pot until golden brown. Add carrots and onions. Cover and cook until tender. Remove from heat. Blend in flour. Stir in milk. Mash half of the potatoes and add rest of the ingredients. Add the other half of the potatoes. Heat until hot enough to serve.

Serves 8

STEPHENSON'S APPLE TREE INN
5755 N.W. Northwood Road
Kansas City, Missouri 64151
(816) 587–9300

▓ Idaho Potato Soup

2 leeks, chopped
2 medium yellow onions,
  chopped
2 tablespoons peanut oil
4 medium baked potatoes,
  chopped and peeled
6 cups chicken stock
Salt and pepper to taste
6 tablespoons sour cream
1/2 cup grated cheddar cheese
1/4 cup cooked and chopped
  bacon
6 green onions, sliced for
  garnish

Sauté leeks and onions in peanut oil until translucent. Add potatoes and cover all with chicken stock. Let simmer for 20 minutes. Season with salt and pepper. Whisk in 1 tablespoon sour cream per serving. Garnish with cheese, bacon, and green onions.

Serves 6

FITZPATRICK'S

❧ Wild Rice Soup

1/4 cup chopped onion
1/2 cup chopped celery
1/2 cup butter
3/4 cup flour
3 cups chicken consommé
1 cup water
3 cups cooked wild rice
1 cup chopped ham
1 cup chopped carrots
1/4 teaspoon salt
1 teaspoon white pepper
1-1/4 teaspoon curry powder
1/2 cup shredded cheddar
   cheese
1 cup half-and-half
1/3 cup sherry

Cook onions and celery in butter until tender. Add flour, stirring well to form a roux. Cook for 5 minutes, stirring occasionally. Combine consommé and water. Slowly add to roux, stirring constantly. Cook on medium heat for 30 minutes, stirring frequently until thickened. Add remaining ingredients and cook for an additional 30 minutes, stirring frequently. Remove and serve.

Serves 8

PARKWAY 600 GRILL
600 Ward Parkway
Kansas City, Missouri 64112
(816) 931-6600

❧ Plaza III Steak Soup

4 tablespoons butter
1/4 cup flour
2 (10-ounce) cans beef
   consommé
1/4 cup diced carrots
1/4 cup diced onions
1/4 cup diced celery
1/2 cup chopped canned
   tomatoes
3/4 teaspoon Kitchen Bouquet
1 beef bouillon cube
1/4 teaspoon ground black
   pepper
5 ounces frozen mixed
   vegetables
1/2 pound ground beef steak,
   browned and drained

Place butter in a soup pot and allow to melt without browning. Add flour and stir to form a roux. Cook the mixture for 3 minutes over medium heat without browning, stirring constantly. Add consommé to the roux and stir until smooth and lightly thickened. Bring to a full boil.

Add the fresh vegetables, tomatoes, and seasonings, and allow to return to boil. Reduce heat and simmer until vegetables are just barely tender (20 to 30 minutes). Add frozen vegetables and ground steak. Simmer an additional 15 minutes. Be sure to cook long enough that the flavors become well blended.

Serves 4

PLAZA III–THE STEAKHOUSE
4749 Pennsylvania
Kansas City, Missouri 64112
(816) 753–0000

❧ Iced Tomato and Watercress Soup

2 tablespoons olive oil
1 medium leek, white part
    only, chopped (reserve green
    part for stock)
1/2 cup chopped yellow onion
2 medium cloves garlic,
    minced
2 cups defatted chicken stock
1 cup peeled and cubed potato
2 large ripe tomatoes, peeled,
    seeded, and chopped
1 cup watercress leaves, firmly
    packed
1 tablespoon minced parsley
Pinch sugar
1/2 cup whipping cream
Salt and freshly ground pepper
    to taste
4 tablespoons sour cream or
    crème fraîche
Additional watercress sprigs
    for garnish
2 teaspoons finely diced
    tomato for garnish

Heat olive oil in medium saucepan over low heat. Add chopped leek, onion, and garlic. Cover and cook until onions are translucent, stirring occasionally, about 10 minutes. Add chicken stock, potato, and tomatoes. Increase heat and bring to a boil, then simmer until potato is tender (10 to 15 minutes). Add watercress leaves, parsley, and sugar, and simmer another 10 minutes. Cool to room temperature. Add whipping cream and puree in food processor. Adjust seasonings to taste.

Garnish with a dollop of sour cream or crème fraîche and fresh watercress. Sprinkle with finely diced tomato meat.

This is an excellent first course for a warm evening.

Serves 4

THE CLASSIC CUP (PLAZA)
310 West 47th Street
Kansas City, Missouri 64112
(816) 753–1009

❧ Vegetarian Minestrone

2 (16-ounce) cans whole peeled
   tomatoes
4 cups water
1/4 cup julienned zucchini
1/4 cup julienned carrots
1/4 cup thinly sliced celery
1/2 cup chopped white onion
2 tablespoons minced garlic
1-1/2 tablespoons chopped
   sweet basil
4 bay leaves
1/4 cup olive oil
1/2 cup white beans,
   precooked
1/2 cup pasta, precooked
2 tablespoons sugar
Salt and white pepper to taste
Fresh grated Parmesan cheese
   to taste

Puree 1 can of tomatoes and place in a heavy 4-quart saucepan. Add the juice from the second can to the saucepan and medium dice the remaining tomatoes. Add these to the saucepan. Pour in the water and then add zucchini, carrots, celery, onion, garlic, basil, bay leaves, and oil. Simmer for 45 minutes, until vegetables are tender.

Add beans, pasta, sugar, salt, and pepper. Simmer an additional 15 minutes. Garnish with Parmesan cheese. (*Note:* This soup may be prepared up to 1 week in advance. Keep covered in the refrigerator.)

Serve with a good crusty Italian or French bread and butter.

Serves 4 to 6

ANDE-LEI'S CAFE

❧ Norma's Bean Soup

1 pound mixed beans
1 teaspoon baking soda
1 cup chopped tomatoes
4 cups chicken stock (or
    vegetable stock)
3 onions, chopped
3 cloves garlic, minced
3 tablespoons chopped parsley
1/4 cup chopped green pepper
4 tablespoons brown sugar
1 teaspoon salt
1 teaspoon crushed bay leaves
1/4 cup vegetable oil
1 teaspoon oregano
1/2 teaspoon ground cumin
    seeds
1/2 teaspoon crushed
    rosemary leaves
1/2 teaspoon celery seed
1/2 teaspoon ground
    marjoram
1/2 teaspoon sweet basil
4 whole cloves
1 cup sherry
Black pepper to taste
Chopped green onion

Soak beans overnight in a large pan filled with water. Drain and cover with fresh water, add baking soda, and bring to a boil. Drain and rinse. Add remaining ingredients except sherry and pepper. Bring to a boil. Cover and cook slowly until beans are tender, about 3 hours. Add sherry and pepper to taste. Garnish with green onion. (*Note:* This recipe is best fixed a day ahead of time, and it can be frozen.)

Serve this hearty fare with corn bread and salad.

Serves 6

ALL WRAPPED UP

❧ Mama's Stuffed Artichokes

8 artichokes
1/2 cup olive oil
1/3 cup chopped onion
1/3 cup chopped celery
1/3 cup chopped mushrooms
3 large cloves garlic, peeled
  and minced
1/4 teaspoon each salt and
  pepper
2 cups unseasoned bread
  crumbs
2 cups shredded Gruyère
  cheese
Melted butter
2 lemons, cut into wedges

Trim artichokes with kitchen scissors, removing spiny ends. Open to the center and, with a spoon, remove the hairy center (the "choke," or tiny layer on top; do not remove heart). Steam for 20 to 30 minutes. Remove and cool.

Heat oil in a sauté pan. Add onion, celery, mushrooms, garlic, salt, and pepper, and cook until soft. Stir in bread crumbs. Let cool briefly. Add cheese and mix thoroughly. Gently pull leaves of artichoke apart and place a small amount of stuffing in each.

Place stuffed artichokes on a cookie sheet. Drizzle with butter and bake for 20 minutes at 375 degrees until centers are hot. Place in small bowl with underliner to catch the leaves as they are eaten. Garnish with lemon wedges and serve at once. (*Note:* Stuffing may be made in advance and stored in the refrigerator until needed.)

Serves 8

MAMA STUFFEATI'S RISTORANTE

❧ Caponata

3 large eggplants
1 stalk celery, diced
1 medium onion, chopped fine
3 tablespoons olive oil
2 cups thick tomato sauce
2 cups balsamic vinegar
1/2 cup sugar
1/4 teaspoon salt
1/8 teaspoon pepper
1/2 pound capers
1 pound green Italian olives,
    pitted and chopped
Oil for frying

Cut eggplant into cubes, but do not peel. Soak in salt water for at least 1 hour. Boil celery; drain and set aside. Sauté onions in olive oil, then add tomato sauce, vinegar, sugar, salt, and pepper. Cook until boiling. Add celery, capers, and olives. Cook for 10 minutes. Drain and dry eggplant, then deep fry until brown. Drain well and stir eggplant into tomato mixture, then cook until it reaches boiling. Remove from stove. Cool overnight and store in refrigerator.

This dish may be served on lettuce leaves as either an appetizer or as a salad, and it can be accompanied by crisp slices of garlic toast and fresh chopped parsley.

Makes 8 cups

CASCONE'S ITALIAN RESTAURANT
3733 North Oak Trafficway
Kansas City, Missouri 64116
(816) 454-7977

❖ Ragout of Fresh Morels and Asparagus

1/4 pound morel mushrooms
Pinch of minced shallots
1 tablespoon butter
1 tablespoon port
1 tablespoon vermouth
1/3 cup heavy cream
16 asparagus spears
1 tomato, julienned
4 parsley sprigs
4 pieces toast

Sauté morels and shallots in butter. Deglaze pan with wines, then add cream and simmer for about 3 minutes. Slice asparagus in 2 sections and put the asparagus heads aside. Add the rest of asparagus to the sauce containing the morels and and cook until tender. Season to taste. For the presentation, garnish with julienned tomatoes and parsley leaves.

Serve the ragout on a square of puff pastry or toast.

Serves 4

LA MEDITERRANÉE
9058-B Metcalf Avenue
Overland Park, Kansas 66212
(913) 341-9595

❧ Greek Feta Cheese Spread

1/2 pound feta cheese,
   crumbled
2 tablespoons olive oil
2 tablespoons muscatel (or any
   sweet wine)
1/4 teaspoon Worcestershire
   sauce
1/2 onion, minced
1 teaspoon parsley
1 teaspoon oregano
1/2 teaspoon pepper
Dash of nutmeg
Pinch of garlic powder
4 pita loaves, cut into quarters
1/4 pound butter, room
   temperature

Rinse feta in cold water to remove excess salt. Combine all ingredients in a bowl and beat with electric mixer at medium speed until creamy, but not whipped. Cover and refrigerate until ready to use.

Butter pita bread and lightly toast in oven. Serve with cheese spread.

Serves 6–10

VETTA'S GRECIAN CUISINE

❧ Puerto Vallarta Wheels

1/4 cup cooked black beans
2 jalapeño peppers, seeded
1 whole pimiento, seeded
1 teaspoon cumin
1/4 bunch cilantro
1/4 teaspoon salt
2 (8-ounce) packages cream
    cheese
2 (10-inch) flour tortillas
Salsa or picante sauce

Combine beans, peppers, pimiento, cumin, cilantro, and salt in a food processor with blade attachment and chop coarsely. Add cream cheese and blend until smooth. Spread mixture on tortillas, roll up, and chill. Remove from refrigerator and cut into 1/2-inch slices. Serve with your favorite salsa or picante sauce.

Serves 6

JOE D'S WINE BAR & CAFE
6227 Brookside Plaza
Kansas City, Missouri 64113
(816) 333–6116

❧ Bayside Beach Crab Cakes

2 pounds crabmeat
2 egg whites
2 cups Homemade
   Mayonnaise
3 cups bread crumbs, fresh and
   fine (reserve 2 cups for
   breading)
2 tablespoons minced celery
2 tablespoons Dijon mustard
2 tablespoons chopped parsley
1 tablespoon minced scallions
1 teaspoon Worcestershire
   sauce
1 teaspoon lemon juice
1/8 teaspoon cayenne pepper
Splash Tabasco
1/2 cup butter

Combine all ingredients except egg whites and crabmeat and mix together. Add egg whites and mix well. Fold in crab and try not to break up. Refrigerate for a while to allow mixture to set up. Remove from refrigerator and form into patties. Bread with remaining 2 cups of bread crumbs. Sauté quickly in butter over high heat until golden brown on both sides. Serve with **Mustard Sauce**.

Serves 8 to 10

Homemade Mayonnaise

4 whole eggs
4 egg yolks
3-1/2 cups peanut oil
2 teaspoons Dijon mustard
2 teaspoons lemon juice
1/2 teaspoon salt and white
   pepper mixed
Dash Tabasco

Combine all ingredients except oil in a food processor. With the motor running, very slowly add a thin stream of oil and continue until all oil has been incorporated. Mayonnaise should be thick and smooth.

Makes about 4 cups

Mustard Sauce

2 cups Homemade
    Mayonnaise
3 tablespoons Dijon mustard
2 tablespoons Pommery
    mustard
1/2 cup sour cream

Combine all ingredients in a stainless steel bowl and blend well.

Makes about 2-1/2 cups

CAFE ALLEGRO
1815 West 39th Street
Kansas City, Missouri 64111
(816) 561-3663

✿ Crabmeat Ravigote

5 cups lump crabmeat
1 head iceberg lettuce,
    shredded

Chill crabmeat and shredded lettuce in refrigerator. Blend crabmeat with **Ravigote Sauce,** being careful not to break up the meat. Chill again in refrigerator. Serve on bed of shredded lettuce.

Serves 6 to 8

Ravigote Sauce

1 cup mayonnaise
1-1/2 tablespoons minced bell
    pepper
1-1/2 tablespoons minced
    green onions
1-1/2 tablespoons minced
    anchovies
1-1/2 tablespoons minced
    pimiento

Combine all ingredients and blend with chilled crabmeat.

Makes 1-1/3 cups

SAVOY GRILL
9th and Central Streets
Kansas City, Missouri 64105
(816) 842–3890

❧ Salmon Ceviche

1 pound fresh salmon,
  boneless
2/3 cup freshly squeezed lime
  juice
1/2 cup orange juice
4 medium tomatoes, peeled,
  seeded, and diced
1 red onion, finely diced
1/2 cup diced sweet red
  pepper
1/3 cup olive oil
1/3 cup coarsely chopped
  fresh cilantro
2 teaspoons seeded and
  minced pickled jalapeño
  peppers
Salt and cayenne pepper to
  taste
Lettuce leaves for garnish
1 cup crumbled tortilla chips

Cube salmon into 1/2-inch pieces. Marinate in lime juice for 30 to 60 minutes. Strain fish from the juice. Place fish in a bowl together with remaining ingredients and gently toss. Taste for seasoning, adding more salt, pepper, cilantro, and other spicy condiments as your palate dictates. Cover and refrigerate 30 to 60 minutes. Serve cold on chilled lettuce leaves. Sprinkle with crumbled tortilla chips.

Serves 4 to 6

THE BISTRO AT THE CLASSIC CUP
4130 Pennsylvania
Kansas City, Missouri 64111
(816) 756–0771

❧ Chilled Grilled Shrimp with Tomato Salsa

1 pound (25–30 per pound)
  green headless shrimp,
  peeled and deveined
3 cups peanut oil
3 cloves fresh garlic, minced
1/4 cup lemon juice
2 tablespoons warm water
2 teaspoons seasoned salt
1/4 teaspoon dried thyme
1/4 teaspoon dried basil
1/4 teaspoon dried oregano
6 large lettuce or kale leaves
1 cup shredded red cabbage
1 bunch cilantro
1 lime, cut into wedges

Stir together peanut oil, garlic, lemon juice, water, salt, thyme, basil, and oregano. Marinate peeled shrimp in this mixture in refrigerator for about 8 hours. Grill marinated shrimp over hot fire for approximately 3 minutes per side or until just cooked through. Spread out cooked shrimp and cool completely.

On a salad-sized plate, cover serving area with leaf lettuce or kale and top with bed of shredded red cabbage. Arrange chilled shrimp on cabbage, and place a cup of **Tomato Salsa** in the center. Garnish with fresh cilantro and wedges of lime. (*Note:* Shrimp can be refrigerated for up to 3 days; salsa for 3 weeks).

Serves 4

Tomato Salsa

1 cup chili sauce
1 cup catsup
1 tablespoon prepared
  horseradish
1 teaspoon lime juice
1 tablespoon chopped fresh
  cilantro
1/2 tablespoon chopped fresh
  parsley
1/4 teaspoon freshly ground
  black pepper
Tabasco to taste
1/2 teaspoon A-1 Sauce

Combine all ingredients, mix well, and chill.

Makes 2 cups

REMINGTON'S
Adam's Mark Hotel, 9103 East 39th Street
Kansas City, Missouri 64133
(816) 737-4733

🪺 Southwest Flyers

4 pounds chicken wings,
  jointed (no tips)
1/2 cup orange juice
2 jalapeño peppers, seeded and
  diced
1-1/2 teaspoons minced garlic
2 cups red wine vinegar
3/4 teaspoon salt
1/2 teaspoon pepper
2 cups salad oil
3 tablespoons chili powder
2 tablespoons ground cumin
1-1/2 teaspoons cayenne
  pepper

Combine orange juice, jalapeños, garlic, vinegar, salt, and pepper in a blender. With motor running slowly, pour in salad oil to make a thick dressing. Place wings in a container with cover, pour marinade over wings. Toss to coat. Marinate at least 4 hours.

Preheat oven to 425 degrees. Combine chili powder, cumin, and cayenne pepper. Remove wings from marinade and place on baking pan. Sprinkle with seasoning mixture. Bake for 15 minutes or until almost done. Remove from oven and cool.

Preheat broiler or grill. Place wings on grill and cook until hot and crisp. Pour **Chili Honey Sauce** over wings and place under broiler to glaze. (*Note*: Wings can be baked in advance and stored in the refrigerator until ready to glaze.)

Serves 8

Chili Honey Sauce

2 cups chicken broth
1/2 cup honey
1-1/4 tablespoons chili powder
1 teaspoon cayenne pepper
1 tablespoon cornstarch
1 cup water

Place chicken broth, honey, chili powder, and cayenne pepper in a saucepan and bring to a boil. Reduce sauce by 1/3. Mix cornstarch with water, add boiling sauce, and cook until sauce is thick enough to coat a spoon. Serve as a glaze for chicken wings or roasted poultry. (*Note*: This dish can be prepared 3 days in advance and stored covered in the refrigerator.)

Makes 3-1/2 cups

PARADISE DINER
11327 West 95th Street
Overland Park, Kansas 66214
(913) 894-2222

❧ Duck Strudel

3 pounds duck meat, chopped
1 pound shitake mushrooms
2 medium leeks, chopped
1/2 cup butter, room
   temperature
4 tablespoons flour
4 cups heavy cream
2 boxes Boursin cheese
2 rolls phyllo dough (8 sheets)
1/2 cup melted butter, plus
   additional 1/2 cup at room
   temperature
Fresh herbs for garnish, such
   as rosemary

Sauté duck meat, mushrooms, and leeks in 1/2 cup of butter. Sprinkle flour into mixture and blend. Add cream and cheese to mixture. Let cool and chill in refrigerator overnight.

Lay out 4 sheets of phyllo flat on cloth or parchment paper. Brush each sheet with 1 tablespoon of melted butter. Place 1/8 of chilled mixture on upper center of dough, fold over sides, then roll. Butter outside of dough heavily. Bake in oven at 425 degrees for 20 minutes or until brown. Repeat steps with phyllo and mixture for remaining rolls. Garnish with fresh herbs. (*Note:* Strudel may be prepared up to 1 day in advance. Store in refrigerator in an airtight container.)

Serves 8

THE PEPPERCORN DUCK CLUB
Hyatt Regency Crown Center, 2345 McGee Street
Kansas City, Missouri 64108
(816) 421-1234

❧ Carpaccio

3/4 pound raw beef
  tenderloin, trimmed of
  silver skin and fat
2 tablespoons finely chopped
  capers
2 tablespoons minced shallots
2 tablespoons minced garlic
1/2 cup olive oil
10 turns of pepper mill of
  cracked black pepper
1 head of romaine lettuce,
  shredded
Additional capers for garnish
Melba toast

Combine capers, shallots, garlic, olive oil, and pepper. Rub spices all over tenderloin and marinate 1 to 2 hours. Wrap meat with plastic wrap and freeze a minimum of 2 hours. Remove beef from freezer and slice paper thin. Lay over bed of shredded romaine. Let sit at room temperature 10 minutes. Drizzle with **Mustard Caper Dressing** and garnish with capers. Serve immediately with melba toast.

Serves 4

Mustard Caper Dressing

1/2 cup of mayonnaise
2 tablespoons finely chopped
  capers
1 tablespoon minced garlic
1 tablespoon Dijon mustard
2 tablespoons dry white wine
Salt and pepper to taste

Combine mayonnaise, capers, garlic, mustard, and wine to creamy consistency. Season with salt and pepper.

Makes about 1 cup

LA SCALLA ITALIAN RESTAURANT

❦ Arancini

1-1/2 pounds ground beef
1 medium onion, minced
1/3 cup tomato paste
1/4 cup water
2 cups uncooked rice (makes
  6 cups cooked rice)
4 eggs
4 cups bread crumbs
1/2 cup grated Romano cheese
1/4 teaspoon salt
1/8 teaspoon pepper
Oil for frying

Brown ground beef and onion together. Add tomato paste and water. Let simmer for about 10 minutes. Season with salt and pepper to taste and set aside to cool.

Cook rice until tender. Drain and cool slightly. While rice is cooking, thoroughly mix 1 cup bread crumbs, 2 eggs, grated Romano, salt, and pepper. Combine bread mixture with cooked rice and mix well.

Place 2 tablespoons of rice mixture in the palm of the hand. Make a well in rice and place about 1 heaping tablespoon of meat into it. Mold rice around meat into the shape of an egg. Dip balls in 2 beaten eggs and roll in remaining 3 cups of bread crumbs. Fry in deep hot oil until golden brown on all sides, about 3 minutes. Do not fry too close together. Remove from oil with a slotted spoon.

This may be served as an appetizer or as a side dish instead of potatoes. As a variation, include a bowl of tomato or marinara sauce for dipping.

Serves 8 (makes about 30 rice balls)

CASCONE'S ITALIAN RESTAURANT
3733 North Oak Trafficway
Kansas City, Missouri 64116
(816) 454–7977

❧ Boudin Balls

2 pounds ground pork
1 cup chopped onion
1 cup chopped scallions
2 tablespoons chopped parsley
1 tablespoon garlic powder
1/4 teaspoon sage
2 tablespoons salt
1/4 teaspoon pepper
1/4 tablespoon cayenne
    pepper
1/4 teaspoon thyme
1/4 teaspoon allspice
1/4 teaspoon mace
2 cups cooked rice
2 eggs

Combine all ingredients except rice and eggs in a skillet. Cook over medium heat until pork in browned. Remove from heat and let cool. Add rice and raw eggs, blending thoroughly. Form into balls approximately 1-1/2 inches in diameter. Roll balls in **Creole Cornmeal** to coat and deep fry until golden brown.

Serves 12 to 16

Creole Cornmeal

2 cups cornmeal
2 tablespoons garlic powder
1/4 teaspoon cayenne
1/4 teaspoon paprika

Mix all ingredients thoroughly and use as a coating.

KIKI'S BON TON MAISON
1515 Westport Road
Kansas City, Missouri 64111
(816) 931–9417

❧ Bruschetta

1 loaf Italian bread, sliced
  2 inches thick
2 cloves garlic, minced
1/2 cup olive oil
2 tomatoes, peeled, seeded,
  and diced
1/2 white onion, diced
6–8 oil-cured black olives,
  chopped fine
1/4 teaspoon salt
1/8 teaspoon red pepper
6–8 fresh basil leaves, cut into
  strips
Anchovy strips (optional)

Add 1 clove minced garlic to olive oil and brush on bread. Place under broiler and toast both sides until golden. In a mixing bowl, combine tomatoes, onion, 1 clove minced garlic, and olives. Drizzle remaining olive oil over this mixture. Add salt, red pepper, and basil, and marinate 2 to 3 hours.

When ready to serve, add 2 to 3 tablespoons tomato mixture to crusty garlic bread. Top with anchovy strips or fresh basil leaf. Serve as an appetizer.

This is also a good spread for sandwiches made with Genoa salami.

Serves 6 to 8

TRATTORIA MARCO POLO
7512 Wornall Road
Kansas City, Missouri 64114
(816) 361–0900

❧ Roast Garlic Spread

2 heads whole garlic
4 sprigs fresh thyme
1/2 teaspoon fresh rosemary
2 cups grated Monterey Jack
  cheese
2–4 tablespoons olive oil
Coarse ground black pepper to
  taste
Pink and green peppercorns
  for garnish

Preheat oven to 350 degrees. Cut heads of garlic in half. Place 2 sprigs fresh thyme and 1/4 teaspoon fresh rosemary between garlic halves. Wrap garlic in two thicknesses of aluminum foil and place in oven for 30 minutes. Remove from oven, unwrap, and let cool. Peel garlic.

Place grated cheese and herb-roasted garlic in a food processor and process briefly. Add ground pepper and 2 tablespoons of olive oil. Process until smooth and creamy, adding more olive oil if necessary. Garnish with pink and green peppercorns.

Serve in a crock or bowl alongside toasted French or sourdough bread or crackers. This spread also is excellent to brush on grilled lamb chops.

Makes 2 cups

CALIFORNOS
4124 Pennsylvania
Kansas City, Missouri 64111
(816) 531–7878

Main Courses

◙ Spanokotyropeta

2 pounds fresh spinach
1 tablespoon salt
3/4 cup olive oil
1 medium onion, finely
　chopped
2 bunches green onions,
　chopped
1 cup chopped parsley
2 leek bulbs, finely chopped
2 pounds feta cheese
1/2 cup dill
3 tablespoons Cavenders
　Greek Seasoning
4 eggs, slightly beaten
1 pound phyllo pastry
1/2 pound butter, melted

Wash spinach and chop. Sprinkle with a little salt and allow to stand 15 minutes. Squeeze spinach to remove excess moisture.

In a large frying pan heat olive oil. Cook onion until gold in color. Add green onions and cook for 3 to 5 minutes. Add spinach and parsley, and cook for 3 minutes. Add leeks and cook 3 to 5 minutes longer. Remove from heat.

Crumble feta and add to spinach mixture, mixing with a fork. Add dill and Greek seasoning, and then fold in the eggs. Grease the bottom of a 10-inch by 15-inch pan. Place 2 phyllo leaves in the bottom of the pan and brush with butter. Continue layering, 1 phyllo leaf at a time, brushing with butter until you have used 12 leaves. Let the pastry cover the sides and corners of the pan like a pie crust. Place the spinach mixture over the layered phyllo and cover with the remaining leaves, 1 at a time, brushing each with butter. Fold all excess phyllo from around the pan and lay them on the top, sealing all edges. Brush with butter. Bake at 350 degrees for 45 minutes or until top is golden.

Serves 8 to 10

VETTA'S GRECIAN CUISINE

◙ Spaghetti Squash Alfredo

1 medium spaghetti squash
1 cup heavy cream
1 cup clarified unsalted butter
1 cup Parmesan cheese
Pinch of white pepper
Pinch of nutmeg
2 tablespoons thinly sliced
    fresh basil or spinach
1/4 cup toasted pine nuts
Coarsely ground black pepper
    to taste

Preheat oven to 350 degrees. Cut squash in half lengthwise. Place cut side down in 3 inches of water in a roasting pan and bake until a knife inserted in the squash meets little resistance (do not overbake). Remove squash from water and cool slightly. Remove seeds by scraping them out. Cover squash loosely with foil and set aside.

Place cream in a medium, heavy-bottomed saucepan. When it begins to simmer, add clarified butter and Parmesan cheese. Whisk constantly until mixture becomes thick and cheese begins to melt. Add white pepper and nutmeg. Let simmer briefly until creamy. Scrape spaghetti squash into Alfredo sauce and stir to coat.

Place a portion of squash on 4 serving plates and garnish with fresh basil or spinach and a sprinkle of toasted pinenuts. Add pepper to taste.

Serves 4

CALIFORNOS
4124 Pennsylvania
Kansas City, Missouri 64111
(816) 531–7878

◙ Spaghettini Napoletana

16 ounces spaghettini, cooked
1/3 cup olive oil
4 whole garlic cloves
4 cups chopped canned Roma
  tomatoes
4 tablespoons chopped fresh
  basil
4 tablespoons minced garlic
Salt and pepper to taste
4 tablespoons grated Romano
  cheese

Heat oil in a large sauté pan. When oil is hot, add garlic cloves and brown slightly. Add tomatoes. Let simmer and stir occasionally. Add basil, garlic, salt, and pepper, and cook for approximately 10 to 15 minutes, stirring occasionally. Reheat cooked pasta in hot water, drain well, and add to the tomatoes, blending well. Add Romano cheese and mix well. Serve at once.

Serves 4

FIGLIO
209 West 46th Terrace
Kansas City, Missouri 64112
(816) 561–0505

⊚ Pasta with Vodka Sauce and Sun-Dried Tomatoes

1 pound penne or other
 tubular pasta
5 tablespoons unsalted butter
1/2 cup julienned sun-dried
 tomatoes
2/3 cup vodka, preferably
 Polish or Russian
1/4 teaspoon hot red pepper
 flakes
1 (16-ounce) can Roma
 tomatoes, drained, seeded,
 and pureed
3/4 cup heavy cream
1/2 teaspoon salt
3/4 cup freshly grated
 Parmesan cheese

In a large pot of boiling, salted water, cook pasta until al dente (tender but still firm), 8 to 10 minutes. Meanwhile melt butter in a large, non-corrodible skillet over moderate heat. Add sun-dried tomatoes and sauté 3 to 5 minutes. Add vodka and pepper flakes, and simmer for 2 minutes. Add pureed tomatoes and cream, simmering for 5 minutes longer. Season with salt. When pasta is done, drain well and add to skillet with the hot sauce. Reduce heat to low, add the cheese, and mix thoroughly. Pour into a heated bowl and serve at once.

Serves 4

TRATTORIA MARCO POLO
7512 Wornall Road
Kansas City, Missouri 64114
(816) 361–0900

⌬ Linguine Con Salmone

1 pound Colavita linguine or
   good durum wheat linguine
1/2 teaspoon salt
4-1/2 tablespoons olive oil
1 medium shallot, minced
2 cloves garlic, minced
2 tablespoons dry white wine
2 tablespoons chopped fresh
   basil
2 cups heavy cream
1/2 cup freshly grated
   Parmesan cheese
1 small ripe tomato (preferably
   Roma), chopped
1/2 pound smoked salmon,
   coarsely chopped
Salt and pepper to taste
1 small scallion, chopped

Add salt and 2 tablespoons of olive oil to boiling water. Add linguine and stir immediately, cooking uncovered until done. Drain pasta in a colander and cool by rinsing with cold water. Toss with 1 tablespoon of olive oil—just enough to coat pasta and keep it from sticking together. Cover with a moist towel and store in the refrigerator until ready to serve.

Sauté shallots and garlic over high heat in 1-1/2 tablespoons of olive oil until translucent. Add wine and reduce until almost dry. Add cream and reduce by half. Add Parmesan cheese and reduce until cream starts to thicken. Add tomato, salmon, and cooked linguine, and toss well. Add salt and pepper. Garnish with scallions and serve immediately.

Only a salad and Italian bread are needed to complete this rich meal, which is best served at cooler times of the year.

Serves 4

LA SCALLA ITALIAN RESTAURANT

◙ Smoked Salmon Pasta

1-1/4 pounds angel hair pasta,
   cooked
1/2 cup olive oil
12 ounces smoked salmon,
   broken into small pieces
1 medium tomato, chopped
2 teaspoons minced fresh
   garlic
1/2 cup roasted pine nuts
2 tablespoons fresh dill (or
   2 teaspoons dried)

Heat oil in a sauté pan. Add all ingredients except pasta and heat slowly. Add pasta and mix together. Divide into 4 portions and serve.

Serves 4

JOE D'S WINE BAR & CAFE
6227 Brookside Plaza
Kansas City, Missouri 64113
(816) 333-6116

⦿ Seafood Sauté and Pasta

1 pound sea scallops
1 pound shrimp, peeled and
   deveined
3 dozen live Maine mussels,
   debearded and washed
1/2 cup olive oil
1/2 cup white wine
2 cloves fresh garlic, minced
1/2 cup chopped fresh basil
1 each green, red, and yellow
   bell peppers, julienned
1 medium yellow onion,
   minced
1 cup sliced medium
   mushrooms
36 ounces pasta, cooked
Zest and juice of 1 lemon
Salt and white pepper to taste
1 cup grated Romano cheese

Over medium-high heat, sauté seafood in approximately 2 tablespoons of olive oil. Cook 2 to 3 minutes or until halfway done. Add wine, garlic, and basil, and reduce heat. Meanwhile, heat remaining oil in another skillet and sauté the vegetables. Place the cooked pasta in a pan of hot water to reheat (do not boil).

When seafood and vegetables are done, combine them and add lemon zest and juice. Season with salt and pepper. Remove from heat. Drain pasta and place in bowls. Carefully arrange seafood and vegetables on top of pasta and pour liquid from pan over all. Top with Romano cheese.

Serves 6

FITZPATRICK'S

ⓠ Chicken and Cheese Pasta

1-1/2 pounds fettucini,
  cooked
1/2 cup cooking oil
1 pound chicken breast, diced
1/4 pound fresh mushrooms,
  sliced
1/4 cup frozen green peas,
  thawed
1/4 cup butter
2 cups heavy cream
3/4 cup grated Parmesan
  cheese
1/4 cup grated mozzarella
  cheese
1/4 cup grated Swiss cheese
Fresh parsley for garnish

Cook pasta and set aside. Heat oil in a large sauté pan. Add chicken and cook until done. Add mushrooms and peas to chicken and toss until mushrooms are tender and peas are heated through. Drain oil, then add butter, cream, and cheeses. Cook over medium heat until sauce is formed. Add fettucini and toss until completely coated. Divide into bowls and sprinkle with fresh parsley.

Garlic toast is just the right "extra" for this dish.

Serves 4 to 6

PARKWAY 600 GRILL
600 Ward Parkway
Kansas City, Missouri 64112
(816) 931–6600

@ Shrimp Coconut

2 pounds medium shrimp
2 teaspoons coriander seeds,
   roasted and ground
1/4 teaspoon fenugreek,
   roasted and ground
1 teaspoon black peppercorns,
   roasted and ground
6 curry leaves (or 1 tablespoon
   curry powder)
2 tablespoons vegetable oil
1 tablespoon black mustard
   seeds
1/4 teaspoon garlic puree
2 teaspoons ginger puree
1 large onion, peeled and cut
   into rings
5 tablespoons coconut milk
1 tablespoon coconut powder
3/4 cup milk
Juice of 1 lemon
1–3 fresh chilies, chopped
   (optional)
Salt to taste
1/4 cup chopped peanuts
1/4 cup chopped tomato
1/4 cup chopped fresh
   coriander

Remove heads, devein, wash, and dry shrimp. Make a paste of coriander, fenugreek, peppercorns, and curry, using a little water. Heat the oil and sauté mustard seeds, garlic, and ginger. Then sauté the spice paste for 1 minute. Add onion rings and sauté until translucent. Add coconut milk, coconut powder, and milk. Stir-fry until milk dissolves. Add lemon juice, chilies, and salt. When simmering, add the shrimp. Stir-fry for 10 minutes. Garnish with chopped nuts, tomato, and coriander. (*Note:* Some of the unusual ingredients used here can be found in gourmet shops and groceries.)

Serves 4

WEST SIDE CAFE
723 Southwest Boulevard
Kansas City, Missouri 64108
(816) 472–0010

ⓠ Grilled Sea Scallops with Pancetta

1-1/2 pounds large fresh sea
   scallops
1 cup olive oil
2 cloves garlic, minced
1 tablespoon cracked black
   pepper
1 tablespoon lemon juice
4 slices pancetta bacon (or 4
   strips smoked regular bacon)

A day in advance, marinate scallops in oil, garlic, pepper, and lemon juice in the refrigerator. Cook bacon until crisp, drain, and set aside. Over a hot fire, place the scallops directly onto the grill and cook for about 4 minutes before turning. If scallops stick, cook them a little longer until they turn easily. After turning, cook long enough to heat through. Spoon **Aioli Sauce** onto a plate and spread around. Arrange scallops on top of the sauce, followed by crumbled bacon.

Serve with fresh vegetables and seasoned boiled potatoes.

Serves 4

Aioli Sauce

2 fresh egg yolks
1 cup olive oil
1 tablespoon lemon juice
2 cloves garlic, minced
2 teaspoons fresh basil (or
   1 teaspoon dried)
Salt and Tabasco to taste
1/2 teaspoon Worcestershire
   sauce
1 teaspoon red wine vinegar
2 anchovy fillets, minced

W hisk egg yolks together and slowly drizzle in the olive oil. If mixture gets too thick, add lemon juice, then thin with a little warm water to a thin mayonnaise consistency. Add the garlic, basil, salt, Tabasco, and Worcestershire sauce. Add vinegar and anchovies. Mix thoroughly and chill.

Makes a little over 1 cup

REMINGTON'S
Adam's Mark Hotel, 9103 East 39th Street
Kansas City, Missouri 64133
(816) 737-4733

Halibut Fillet with Red Pepper Beurre Blanc

4–6 (7–8-ounce) halibut fillets

Sauté, poach, or bake fillets until done (approximately 6 to 10 minutes, depending on thickness). Top with **Beurre Blanc** and serve.

Serves 4

Beurre Blanc

1/2 cup white wine
1 tablespoon tarragon vinegar
1 shallot, diced
1 medium red pepper,
    chopped
1/4 cup heavy cream
1 cup unsalted butter, chilled
Salt to taste

Combine wine, vinegar, shallot, and red pepper. Bring to a slow boil and reduce until 2 tablespoons of liquid remain. Add cream and boil for 2 minutes. Lower heat and whisk in butter a little at a time until all butter is incorporated. Remove from heat and place sauce in blender on medium speed for 1 minute. Strain, then season with salt.

JOE D'S WINE BAR & CAFE
6227 Brookside Plaza
Kansas City, Missouri 64113
(816) 333–6116

◙ Golden Potato-Crusted Snapper with Braised Wild Mushrooms and Red Pepper Vinaigrette

2 large potatoes
3/4 cup plus 2 tablespoons
  extra virgin olive oil
Salt and white pepper to taste
Juice of 1 lime
2 tablespoons julienned fresh
  basil leaves
4 (6-ounce) red snapper fillets
1/2 cup sliced wild
  mushrooms (preferably
  morels or shitakes)
2 teaspoons minced shallots
1/4 cup water

Peel and wash potatoes, then thinly slice (1/16-inch thick). Cut potato slices with a round biscuit cutter (3/4-inch in diameter) to create "fish scales." Toss potato slices in 2 tablespoons of oil and season with salt and pepper. Combine lime juice, 2 tablespoons of oil, and 1 tablespoon of basil, and brush over fish fillets. Starting at the head of each fillet, create overlappinng rows of potato "scales." When fillets are completely covered, paint the potatoes with 2 tablespoons more oil, and refrigerate for at least 2 hours.

Preheat oven to 400 degrees. In a large nonstick skillet, fry fish in two batches. Use 3 tablespoons of oil each time. Brown the potato side first. After both sides are browned, place on baking tray and bake for 5 minutes.

Sauté mushrooms and shallots in 2 tablespoons of oil. Add remaining basil. Add water and braise mushrooms until soft. Season to taste with salt and pepper. Spoon 4 tablespoons **Red Pepper Vinaigrette** onto each of 4 plates. Top with snapper and garnish with mushrooms.

Serves 4

Red Pepper Vinaigrette

2 red peppers, roasted, peeled,
  and seeded
1 teaspoon roasted and minced
  garlic
1 shallot, minced
2 teaspoons honey
2 tablespoons champagne
  vinegar
4 teaspoons chopped fresh
  basil
1/3 cup vegetable oil,
  preferably canola
1/3 cup extra virgin olive oil
2–3 tablespoons water
Salt and white pepper to taste

Place peppers, garlic, shallot, honey, vinegar, and basil in a blender. While blending, add oil in a slow stream. Continue blending until very smooth. Thin slightly with water. Add salt and pepper.

Makes 1 cup

THE AMERICAN RESTAURANT
200 East 25th Street, Crown Center
Kansas City, Missouri 64108
(816) 426-1133

◙ Pescado Yucateco

6–8 red snapper fillets
1/2 cup fresh orange juice
1/4 cup fresh lime juice
1/2 teaspoon salt
1/2 teaspoon cracked black
  pepper
4 tablespoons olive oil
2 limes, cut into wedges

Blend juices, spices, and oil to make a marinade. Add red snapper fillets and marinate 4 to 6 hours covered in the refrigerator. Grill over medium-hot coals for about 4 minutes on each side. Serve with **Olive and Red Pepper Sauce** and a wedge of lime.

Serve this tangy combination with **Shredded Romaine Salad** *(recipe on p. 4) and steamed rice.*

Serves 6 to 8

Olive and Red Pepper Sauce

4 tablespoons olive oil
1/2 cup diced white onion
2/3 cup quartered pimiento-
  stuffed olives
1/4 cup julienned red bell
  pepper
2 tablespoons chopped fresh
  cilantro
2 teaspoons minced garlic
1/2 teaspoon bijol (optional)
1/2 cup freshly squeezed
  orange juice
1/4 cup freshly squeezed lime
  juice
2-1/2 tablespoons seafood
  remoulade sauce (Available
  at gourmet stores.)
2 tablespoons dark vermouth
Salt and freshly ground black
  pepper to taste

Sauté onion in olive oil until transluscent. Add olives, red pepper, cilantro, and garlic, and simmer until tender. Add bijol, juices, seafood remoulade, and vermouth. Adjust taste with salt and pepper. Simmer uncovered and reduce most of the liquid. (*Note:* Sauce may be prepared up to 3 days in advance and stored in the refrigerator.)

Makes about 2-1/2 cups

ANDE-LEI'S CAFE

@ Salmon in Parchment

4 salmon steaks, 1-1/2 inch
  thick
1 red pepper, julienned
1 cup snow peas
1 cup julienned carrots
1/2 cup julienned jicama
1/2 cup julienned leeks
Parchment paper

Cut 4 15-inch by 15-inch rectangles of parchment paper and fold each in half. Combine vegetables. Unfold 1 sheet of parchment and place 1 cup of vegetable mixture on 1/2 the paper. Place a salmon steak on top of vegetables. Put 1 teaspoon **Herb Butter** on top of salmon steak. Brush edges of paper lightly with olive oil all around salmon and vegetables.

Fold the empty side of the rectangle over the food and lightly press down around the edges. Beginning on the right side, roll paper tightly up to within 1 inch of the fish and vegetables. Press and roll tightly the edges of the paper all around the fish. You should end up with a half-moon shape. Proceed with remaining salmon steaks and vegetables, using the same process. Brush 2 baking sheets lightly with olive oil and place 2 packets on each. Bake at 500 degrees for 6 minutes.

Place each packet on a dinner plate and cut a small "X" in the top of the paper, folding back edges of the "X" to let the aroma escape. Serve at once.

Serves 4

Herb Butter

1/4 cup unsalted butter,
  softened
1/4 teaspoon dried basil
1/4 teaspoon dried tarragon
Pinch of dried thyme
Pinch of dried oregano

Mix together all ingredients and set aside until ready to use.

Makes 1/4 cup

CALIFORNOS
4124 Pennsylvania
Kansas City, Missouri 64111
(816) 531-7878

◨ Egyptian Salmon

8 (6-ounce) salmon fillets
1/2 cup fresh lemon juice
2 large tomatoes, diced
2 large cucumbers, peeled,
    seeded, and diced
2 large white onions, diced
1 green bell pepper, diced
1 red bell pepper, diced
1 cup chopped fresh parsley
2 teaspoons virgin olive oil
1/2 teaspoon salt
1/2 teaspoon ground black
    pepper
Lemon and orange slices for
    garnish
Parsley for garnish

Combine all ingredients except salmon. Cut eight 8-inch by 10-inch pieces of foil and place a salmon fillet on each. Top salmon evenly with vegetable mix, then wrap foil tightly around fish and vegetables to steam. Charbroil for 8 minutes, or bake in a 350-degree oven for 12 minutes. Garnish serving plates with lemon and orange slices and sprigs of parsley. (*Note:* This dish tastes best with fresh charbroiled salmon.)

This succulent fish is delicious with saffron rice or rice pilaf.

Serves 8

CAFE NILE
8433 Wornall Road
Kansas City, Missouri 64114
(816) 361-9097

▣ Salmon with Hazelnut Lime Butter

4 (6–8-ounce) salmon steaks
4 tablespoons oil
Salt and pepper to taste

Coat salmon with oil and season with salt and pepper. Grill over hot coals approximately 3 to 5 minutes on each side. Serve with a dollop of **Hazelnut Lime Butter.**

Serves 4

Hazelnut Lime Butter

1/4 cup hazelnuts
Zest of 1 lime
Juice of 1/2 lime
1/4 cup unsalted butter,
    softened

Spread hazelnuts on a cookie sheet and place in a 350-degree oven to toast for about 5 minutes. Watch carefully to avoid burning. Finely grind hazelnuts in a food processor. Combine with lime zest, juice, and butter. (*Note:* This keeps in the refrigerator for 3 to 4 days. Bring to room temperature before serving.)

Makes 1/2 cup

CALIFORNOS
4124 Pennsylvania
Kansas City, Missouri 64111
(816) 531–7878

✪ Pepper Tuna

4 (6–8-ounce) fresh tuna steaks
4 tablespoons pink
    peppercorns
4 tablespoons green
    peppercorns
1 lemon, cut into wedges

Crush together pink and green pepper-corns and use to coat the surface of each tuna steak. Grill to taste over hot coals for approximately 2-1/2 minutes each side. Serve with lemon wedges.

Serves 4

CALIFORNOS
4124 Pennsylvania
Kansas City, Missouri 64111
(816) 531–7878

◙ Grilled Tuna Niçoise with Balsamic Vinaigrette

4 (6-ounce) fresh tuna steaks
4 butter lettuce leaves
1 tomato, cut into 8 wedges
1 lime, cut into 8 wedges
1 lemon, cut into 8 wedges
2 cups snow peas, blanched
    (1/2 cup per person)
8 cooked new potatoes, room
    temperature
4 black olives

Prepare grill to a medium-high heat. Be sure to coat the grill grid with a food release so that fish will not stick to the surface. Grill the tuna steaks medium rare, about 2-1/2 minutes per side. (Tuna can easily be overdone; steaks are done when red flesh turns white.)

On 4 large plates, arrange lettuce leaves, tomato wedges, and lemon and lime wedges. Fan snow peas on one side of the plate. Halve the new potatoes and place 4 pieces on each plate. Place the cooked tuna steaks on the lettuce leaves. Drizzle the **Balsamic Vinaigrette** over all and serve.

Serves 4

Balsamic Vinaigrette

1/2 cup balsamic vinegar
1/4 cup olive oil
1 large shallot, minced
1/2 teaspoon black pepper

Combine ingredients and set aside until ready to use.

Makes 3/4 cup

CALIFORNOS
4124 Pennsylvania
Kansas City, Missouri 64111
(816) 531-7878

⊡ Chicken Cacciatore Savina Marie

1 (2-1/2–3-pound) chicken,
  cut up
1/4 cup olive oil
1 medium onion, halved and
  sliced
1 large green pepper, halved
  and sliced
1 clove garlic, minced
1 cup sliced fresh mushrooms
1/2 cup Burgundy
2 (16-ounce) cans whole
  tomatoes
1 tablespoon sugar
1/4 cup chopped fresh parsley
3/4 teaspoon crushed Italian
  seasoning
1/2 teaspoon salt
1/4 teaspoon black pepper
1 pound mostaccioli, cooked
1/4 cup chopped fresh basil

Brown chicken in olive oil. Remove chicken to Dutch oven or large casserole dish with cover. Sauté onion, green pepper, garlic, and mushrooms in same skillet, and cook until all are tender. Add wine and bring to a boil. Chop tomatoes and add them with their juice to the skillet mixture. Add sugar, parsley, Italian seasoning, salt, and pepper. Simmer covered for 20 minutes, stirring occasionally. Pour sauce over chicken and simmer over low heat for 1 hour until chicken is cooked. Serve chicken over pasta with plenty of sauce and top with fresh basil.

Serves 4 to 6

JOHNNY CASCONE'S ITALIAN RESTAURANT
6863 West 91st Street
Overland Park, Kansas 66212
(913) 381–6837

ℚ Chicken Georgina

4 (6-ounce) chicken breasts,
   boned and skinned
1 cup light vegetable oil
2 teaspoons cracked black
   pepper
2 teaspoons salt
2 teaspoons granulated garlic
1 cup sliced mushrooms
1 tablespoon butter
1 clove garlic, minced
2 cups fresh broccoli florets
   (or 1 box frozen)
Grated Parmesan cheese
Paprika
Parsley for garnish

Marinate chicken breasts 3 to 4 hours in a mixture of vegetable oil, pepper, salt, and garlic. Remove breasts and broil approximately 2 minutes on each side until done.

Sauté sliced mushrooms in butter and garlic. Steam broccoli florets. Spoon sautéed mushrooms on chicken breasts, top each breast with 1/2 cup broccoli florets. Top with desired amount of **Beer Cheese Sauce,** following by a sprinkling of grated Parmesan cheese and paprika. Place under broiler and brown. Garnish each breast with a large parsley sprig.

This is delicious served with melon slices, such as crenshaw, honeydew, or cantaloupe.

Serves 4

Beer Cheese Sauce

1/2 cup butter
1 cup all purpose flour
1 cup half-and-half
1/2 cup chicken stock
1/2 cup shredded cheddar
   cheese
White pepper to taste
1/4 cup beer (room
   temperature)

Make a roux by mixing butter and flour in a saucepan, then cooking over medium flame (or medium setting on electric range), stirring constantly, until lightly browned.

Combine cream, chicken stock, and white pepper. Heat to just under boiling point, then reduce heat. Add roux to this mixture 1 tablespoon at a time, mixing well each time with wire whisk, to desired thickness. Add shredded cheese and mix well until cheese is completely melted and incorporate into sauce. Add beer and mix well.

Makes about 3-3/4 cups

CHAPPELL'S RESTAURANT & LOUNGE
323 Armour Road
North Kansas City, Missouri 64116
(816) 471–4400

© Chicken Sicilian

4 chicken breasts, boned and
　skinned
1/4 cup olive oil
2 tablespoons minced garlic
2 tablespoons chopped shallots
1 cup diced tomatoes
1 cup whole black olives
2 cups julienned red bell
　pepper
2 cups julienned green bell
　pepper
2 tablespoons chopped fresh
　thyme
2 tablespoons chopped fresh
　basil
1/4 cup chicken broth
1 pound linguini, cooked

Grill or broil chicken breasts. While chicken is cooking, heat oil in a large sauté pan. Add garlic and shallots, and cook until soft. Add diced tomatoes, black olives, julienned peppers, and herbs, and sauté until hot but still crisp. Pour vegetables into a bowl and set aside until ready to serve. In the same pan, pour in chicken broth and add cooked linguini. Heat thoroughly.

Divide linguini equally among 4 plates. Place a chicken breast on top of pasta, then divide vegetables equally over each breast.

Round out this creation with a salad or side dish.

Serves 4

COYOTE GRILL
4843 Johnson Drive
Mission, Kansas 66205
(913) 362–3333

◙ Lime-Grilled Breast of Chicken

2 (5–6 ounce) chicken breasts,
   boned and skinned
1 teaspoon olive oil
2 tablespoons Dijon mustard
2 tablespoons honey
1/2 teaspoon toasted
   coriander seeds, crushed
Dash pepper
1 fresh lime, half thinly sliced
   and half cut into wedges
2 sprigs fresh cilantro

Coat the chicken breasts with olive oil and sear on a hot grill. Remove from grill and set aside. Combine mustard, honey, coriander seeds, and pepper. Coat chicken with this combination, cover with thinly sliced lime, and place uncovered in a 350-degree oven for about 15 minutes. Garnish each breast with a lime wedge and a sprig of fresh cilantro.

Serves 2

THE BISTRO AT THE CLASSIC CUP
4130 Pennsylvania
Kansas City, Missouri 64111
(816) 756-0771

✆ Grilled Chicken with Mango-Avocado Salsa

12 (4-ounce) chicken breasts,
    boned and skinned
1-1/2 cups white wine
Juice of 1 lemon
Juice of 1 orange
2 tablespoons vegetable oil
2 tablespoons black
    peppercorns
1 tablespoon fresh rosemary
2 teaspoons chopped fresh
    basil
3 bay leaves

Combine all ingredients and marinate chicken in this mixture 4 to 6 hours before grilling. Dredge chicken breasts in additional vegetable oil. Grill over medium heat until cooked through, approximately 10 to 20 minutes. Serve chicken breasts atop **Mango-Avocado Salsa.**

Serves 6

Mango-Avocado Salsa

3 medium mangoes, diced
6 tablespoons finely diced
    green bell pepper
6 tablespoons finely diced red
    bell pepper
2 tablespoons chopped cilantro
    leaves
2 teaspoons chopped chives
2 teaspoons salt
3 teaspoons ground black
    pepper
1 tablespoon olive oil
6 tablespoons minced onion
3 tablespoons champagne
    vinegar
1/4 cup sugar
1 large avocado

Mix mango, green and red peppers, cilantro, chives, salt, pepper, and olive oil in a bowl and set aside. Over medium heat, bring onion, vinegar, and sugar to a boil. Pour hot mixture over ingredients in bowl and toss together. Dice and add avocado just before serving. Season to taste.

Makes 3–4 cups

THE AMERICAN RESTAURANT
200 East 25th Street, Crown Center
Kansas City, Missouri 64108
(816) 426–1133

Ⓠ Baked Chicken 'n' Butter and Cream

8 pieces frying chicken
2 cups flour
1 tablespoon salt
1 tablespoon black pepper
2 teaspoons paprika
1 stick butter, cut into 8 pats
2 cups half-and-half or cream

Dip chicken in cold water. Mix together flour, salt, pepper, and paprika. Coat each piece of chicken thoroughly in flour mixture. Place pieces skin side up in a 13-inch by 9-inch by 2-inch baking dish. Bake uncovered at 450 degrees for 30 minutes or until brown. (Recipe may be prepared ahead up to this point.) Pour cream around chicken, place 1 pat of butter on each piece, and bake at 350 degrees for 45 minutes.

Serve this old-fashioned chicken with fresh corn on the cob and sliced tomatoes.

Serves 8

STEPHENSON'S OLD APPLE FARM RESTAURANT
16401 East 40 Highway
Kansas City, Missouri 64136
(816) 373–5400

◙ Breast of Chicken Oskar

4 (6-ounce) chicken breasts,
    skinned and boned
3/4 cup clarified butter
Seasoned flour, as needed
16 asparagus spears, blanched
    and hot
4 ounces snow crab leg meat,
    cooked
4 sprigs of watercress

Place clarified butter in a small sauté pan and heat until smoking. Dredge chicken in flour and place in sauté pan. Cook crisp on both sides. Place 2 **Holland Rusks** in the center of 4 serving plates and top with a chicken breast. Arrange asparagus spears at border on either side of chicken breast, then top with crab legs in center. Ladle hot **Béarnaise Sauce** over all and garnish with watercress.

Serves 4

Holland Rusks

8 slices white sourdough bread
4 tablespoons melted butter

Remove bread crusts and cut into 4-inch ovals. Brush both sides with butter. Toast on a baking sheet in a 350-degree oven until golden brown and crisp. Hold at room temperature until ready to serve. Do not refrigerate.

Béarnaise Sauce

1/2 cup dry white wine
1/2 cup tarragon vinegar
2 tablesoons dried tarragon
1/2 tablespoon minced
  shallots
1/4 teaspoon black pepper
3 egg yolks
2 tablespooons water
1 cup unsalted butter, hot,
  melted
1-1/2 tablespoons chopped
  fresh tarragon
1/2 tablespoon chopped
  parsley
1/2 teaspoon kosher salt
1/4 teaspoon Tabasco

In a saucepan combine wine, vinegar, tarragon, shallots, and pepper, and cook over medium-high heat until reduced by a third. Store covered in refrigerator until ready to use. Combine egg yolks, 2 tablespoons of tarragon reduction, and water in a stainless steel bowl. Whip over double boiler until volume quadruples and mixture becomes foamy and thick. Drizzle melted butter in slowly. Season to taste with salt and Tabasco, and then garnish with tarragon and parsley.

Makes 4 cups

FEDORA CAFE & BAR
210 West 47th Street
Kansas City, Missouri 64112
(816) 561–6565

ℚ Chicken Broccoli Skillet

1 pound chicken breasts,
  skinned and boned
Diet salt and pepper to taste
2 tablespoons margarine
1/2 cup diced onions
1-1/2 cups cut broccoli
1 teaspoon lemon juice
1/2 teaspoon thyme,
  preferably fresh
3 medium tomatoes, diced
1/2 cup low-sodium tomato
  juice

Cut chicken into 1/2-inch strips and season with salt and pepper. Sauté chicken in margarine. Add onions and continue to cook. Add broccoli, lemon juice, thyme, tomatoes, tomato juice, and simmer approximately 10 to 15 minutes. Serve hot.

This is a light and healthy recipe, only 312 calories.

Serves 4

THE COFFEE SHOP
Kansas City Marriott Downtown
200 West 12th Street
Kansas City, Missouri 64105
(816) 421-6800

▣ Breast of Chicken with Corn Bread Date Stuffing and Madeira Wine Sauce

4 (10-ounce) chicken breasts,
    boned (skinned, optional)
1-1/2 cups corn bread crumbs
16 dates, diced
4 eggs
Salt and pepper to taste
4 tablespoons butter

Pound out chicken breasts slightly, making sure thickness is uniform. Prepare corn bread crumbs using a standard corn bread recipe of your choice. Mix crumbs with dates and eggs. Season with salt and pepper. Place 1/4 of the mixture in the center of each flattened breast. Roll up each and tie with butcher's twine. Sauté in a hot pan with butter, browning skin evenly. Place in a 350-degree oven and bake for 10 minutes. Let rest for 3 minutes. Remove string, slice, and serve with **Madeira Wine Sauce.**

Serves 4

Madeira Wine Sauce

4 strips bacon
4 shallots, minced
1 cup Madeira
2 cups veal stock (may
    substitute beef stock)

Cook bacon in a hot pan until well done. Crumble finely and set aside. Drain all but 1 tablespoon of bacon grease from pan. Add finely chopped shallot and sauté until translucent. Add Madeira and simmer for 1 minute. Add stock and simmer for 3 minutes. Strain and serve warm over chicken.

Makes 1-1/2 cups

THE CAFE AT THE RITZ-CARLTON, KANSAS CITY
401 Ward Parkway
Kansas City, Missouri 64112
(816) 756–1500

ⓠ Bon Ton Poulet

3 chicken breasts, split
1/2 cup melted butter
2 cups chopped onions
1 cup flour
4 cloves garlic, minced
2 cups white wine
4 cups chicken broth
2 teaspoons tomato paste
6 stalks celery, chopped
1 cup sliced black olives
1-1/2 cup chopped
   mushrooms
1 teaspoon thyme
6 cups cooked white rice
1 tomato, cut into 6 wedges
6 sprigs parsley

Brown breasts in melted butter. Set chicken aside and add onions to pan, cooking until transparent. Add flour and reduce heat, stirring flour until it is light brown (3 to 5 minutes). Add chicken and remaining ingredients except rice, tomato wedges, and parsley. Simmer for 35 minutes. Serve breasts over a bed of rice, garnished with parsley sprigs and a wedge of tomato. (*Note:* This dish may be prepared ahead of time and refrigerated. Simply reheat when ready to serve.)

Serves 6

KIKI'S BON TON MAISON
1515 Westport Road
Kansas City, Missouri 64111
(816) 931–9417

ⓠ Pheasant Madeira

4 pheasant breasts, boned and
   skinned
2 cups flour
2 eggs
1 cup buttermilk
1/4 cup butter
1/2 cup Madeira
1 cup sliced shitake
   mushrooms
1/4 cup sliced artichoke
   bottoms
3 cups chicken stock
1 cup heavy cream
1/4 cup halved red grapes

Dredge pheasant breasts in flour. Combine eggs and buttermilk. Dip pheasant into egg mixture. Dredge again. Melt butter and sauté pheasant over medium heat. Cook approximately 4 to 5 minutes on each side. Place in a warm oven to hold.

Heat wine to boiling in a saucepan and add mushrooms. When wine is reduced by half, add artichoke bottoms, chicken stock, and heavy cream. Reduce by half or until thickened to a creamy consistency. Add grapes to sauce at the last minute.

Place a pheasant breast on each plate and pour about 1/4 cup of the sauce over the top of each.

This dish is especially good served with a mixture of white and wild rice seasoned with fresh thyme and diced onions. Carrots that have been steamed and glazed with a mixture of honey and orange juice also go well with this meal. Serve in the fall and winter months when pheasant is usually plentiful.

Serves 4

E.B.T. RESTAURANT
1310 Carondelet Drive
Kansas City, Missouri 64114
(816) 942–8870

@ Duck Provençale

1 domestic duck, cleaned and
  dressed
2 cloves garlic
1 bunch parsley
2 tablespoons Dijon mustard
Salt and pepper to taste
1 cup butter
1 cup white wine

Chop garlic and parsley together. Add mustard. Salt and pepper duck inside and outside cavity. Baste with garlic mixture. Roast 35 minutes at 500 degrees. Cool and debone, leaving breast and legs whole.

To prepare stock, take juice from the roasted duck and add butter, wine, and duck pieces. Heat. Pour sauce over breast and legs.

Try this succulent bird with an accompaniment of wild rice.

Serves 2 to 4

LA MEDITERRANÉE
9058-B Metcalf Avenue
Overland Park, Kansas 66212
(913) 341-9595

ℚ Rack of Lamb with Raspberry Mint Sauce

1 (8-rib) rack of lamb
1/4 teaspoon oregano
2 tablespoons chopped fresh
    rosemary
2 teaspoons salt
1/4 teaspoon ground allspice
3 large cloves garlic, finely
    chopped
1 teaspoon ground black
    pepper
1/2 teaspoon dried leaf thyme
Peel of 2 lemons, finely grated
1-1/2 cups Flower of the
    Flames Raspberry Barbecue
    Sauce (available at gourmet
    shops and through Eddy's
    Catering)
3 tablespoons mint sauce

Have butcher trim rack of lamb, removing all visible fat and the extra, thin flap of meat on the end of the rib. Also have butcher cut through the chime bone. Cut and scrape meat from between long rib bones, leaving 2 to 3 inches of clean bone protruding. Cover exposed bone with a double layer of foil to keep from burning.

In a small bowl, combine oregano, rosemary, salt, allspice, garlic, pepper, thyme, and lemon peel. Rub mixture over surface of meat, then cover and refrigerate at least 2 hours.

Prepare grill, adding apple and pecan wood chips to coals. Place lamb on grill at opposite end from coals and smoke for 1-1/2 to 2 hours. Fire should be at about 240 degrees.

Mix raspberry barbecue sauce and mint sauce in a saucepan and simmer for 10 minutes. Serve warm with lamb.

Serves 4

EDDY'S CATERING
320 North McGee
Kansas City, Missouri 64116
(816) 842-7484

◙ Stuffed Veal Cutlets aux Quatre Fromages

8 very thin veal cutlets
 (2 ounces each)
Salt and pepper to taste
4 slices Swiss cheese
1 cup Rondele cheese (may
 substitute Boursin cheese)
3 eggs
1/2 cup milk
1 cup fine French bread
 crumbs
1 cup finely grated Parmesan
 cheese
1 cup flour
1/2 cup oil

Lay 4 pieces of veal out on work surface and season with salt and pepper. Fold Swiss cheese slices in half and place in middle of cutlets. Top Swiss cheese with 4 tablespoons of Rondele cheese per cutlet. Top with remaining cutlets and tuck under to seal thoroughly. Place in freezer for 2 hours to facilitate breading. Whip eggs and milk together for egg wash. Set aside. Combine bread crumbs and Parmesan cheese and set aside.

Preheat oven to 350 degrees. Remove frozen veal from freezer and dip each cutlet first in flour, then in egg mixture, then in cheese crumb mixture. Press crumbs firmly into the meat. Place veal in large metal-handled skillet over medium heat and brown in oil on both sides. Drain oil and place skillet in oven for 12 to 15 minutes or until the cheese starts to melt out from the sides. Place cutlets on serving plates and ladle **Basil Camembert Butter** over each side.

Serve this rich combination with the vegetable or potato of your choice.

Serves 4

Basil Camembert Butter

1 cup dry white wine
1 cup heavy cream
1 tablespoon minced shallots
1 teaspoon minced garlic
2 ounces (1/4 cup) Camembert
  cheese, rind removed and
  cut in pieces
1/2 cup butter, chilled
2 tablespoons coarsely
  chopped fresh basil

In a heavy saucepan, cook wine, cream, shallots, and garlic over medium-high heat until reduced by half. Lower heat and blend in pieces of cheese. Remove from heat. Cut chilled butter into tablespoon-sized pieces and add to sauce, blending well. Add basil. Keep in a warm place before serving. (*Note*: Preparing sauce an hour ahead ensures fullest flavor.)

Makes 2-3/4 cups

RAPHAEL RESTAURANT
The Raphael Hotel, 325 Ward Parkway
Kansas City, Missouri 64112
(816) 756–3800

✿ Veal Scallopini and Peppers

8 (2-ounce) veal cutlets
2 teaspoons vegetable oil
2 tablespoons flour
1/2 cup sliced onion
1/2 cup sliced mushrooms
1/2 cup sliced green peppers
2 teaspoons basil, preferably
   fresh
Salt and pepper to taste
1/2 cup tomato, peeled,
   seeded, and chopped
1 tablespoon grated Parmesan
   cheese

Flatten veal with a wooden mallet. Heat vegetable oil in skillet. Lightly dust veal with flour and sauté until lightly browned. Turn and cook for about 2 minutes. Remove veal, then add onion, mushrooms, green peppers, basil, salt, and pepper, and continue to cook. Add chopped tomatoes. Cook about 5 minutes. Add veal and simmer. Sprinkle with Parmesan cheese.

This light and healthy recipe is only about 230 calories.

Serves 4

THE COFFEE SHOP
Kansas City Marriott Downtown
200 West 12th Street
Kansas City, Missouri 64105
(816) 421-6800

Q Veal Lemonata

8 (2–3 ounce) veal cutlets
Salt and freshly ground pepper
   to taste
1 eggplant, peeled and sliced
   into eight 1/4-inch rounds
Flour for dredging
2 eggs, lightly beaten
1 cup fresh bread crumbs
1/2 cup plus 3 tablespoons oil
1 tablespoon butter
8 thin, seeded lemon slices
1 teaspoon fresh oregano
1 tablespoon chopped parsley

Pound meat lightly with a flat mallet and sprinkle with salt and pepper. Also sprinkle the eggplant rounds with salt and pepper. Dredge eggplant in flour and shake off excess. Dip in egg, then in bread crumbs. Pat to help the crumbs adhere. Heat the 1/2 cup of oil and sauté eggplant slices on both sides until golden. Drain on paper towels.

Dip the pieces of veal in flour and shake off excess. Dip in egg and coat each piece well. Heat the 3 tablespoons of oil and the butter in a skillet and sauté the veal until golden on both sides.

Arrange the veal on a platter, with slices slightly overlapping. Top each slice with an eggplant round and lemon slice. Sprinkle with oregano and parsley and serve hot.

Serves 4

JASPER'S ITALIAN RESTAURANT
405 West 75th Street
Kansas City, Missouri 64114
(816) 363-3003

◙ Parmesan-Crusted Veal Chop

4 (12–14-ounce) veal rib chops
Salt and lemon pepper to taste
8 eggs
1/4 cup oil
2 cups fine, dry bread crumbs
2 cups grated Parmesan cheese
1 tablespoon garlic powder
1 teaspoon white pepper
1 cup seasoned flour (seasoned
   with salt and white pepper)
1/2 cup melted butter

Lightly season each veal chop on both sides with salt and lemon pepper. Mix together eggs and oil to make egg wash. Set aside. Combine bread crumbs, Parmesan cheese, garlic powder, and white pepper. Set aside. Place each veal chop in seasoned flour, shake off excess. Dip the chops into the egg wash and then into Parmesan crumbs to coat well. Set aside. Place a sauté pan on the stove to heat. Add butter, but do not brown. When hot, add the veal and brown lightly on both sides. Place chops in a 400-degree oven for 12 minutes, or until done.

Serve chops with your favorite tomato sauce or brown sauce.

Serves 4

PLAZA III-THE STEAKHOUSE
4749 Pennsylvania
Kansas City, Missouri 64112
(816) 753-0000

@ Veal Lemonada

8 (2-ounce) veal scallops
1 cup flour
2 eggs, beaten
1/4 teaspoon pepper
1/2 teaspoon salt
1/2 teaspoon seasoned salt
1/4 teaspoon MSG (optional)
2 tablespoons parsley flakes
Lemon pepper to taste
4 tablespoons butter
2 tablespoons olive oil

Dry veal thoroughly and place between 2 pieces of waxed paper. Pound to a thickness of 1/4 inch. Dredge meat in 1/2 cup of flour. Dip in beaten eggs. Dredge in seasoned flour made by combining 1/2 cup flour, pepper, salts, MSG, and parsley flakes, pressing mixture in with finger tips. Sprinkle both sides with lemon pepper. Place butter and oil in skillet over medium-high heat. Sauté veal 3 minutes on one side and 2-1/2 minutes on the other. Remove from pan. Ladle **Butter and White Wine Sauce** over the scallops.

Serves 8

Butter and White Wine Sauce

2-1/2 tablespoons lemon juice
1/4 cup dry white wine
3 tablespoons unsalted butter
3 tablespooons heavy cream

Deglaze skillet used for veal with lemon juice and white wine. Add butter and cream, cooking and stirring constantly until slightly thickened.

Makes about 3/4 cup

MICHAEL FORBES GRILL
7539 Wornall Road
Kansas City, Missouri 64114
(816) 444-5445

@ R.C.'s Skillet Meat Loaf

3 pounds ground beef
1/2 large onion, chopped
3 eggs, slightly beaten
2 cups bread, torn into small
    pieces
3/4 cup tomato sauce
1 tablespoon pepper
1-1/2 teaspoon salt
1-1/2 teaspoon MSG
    (optional)
Catsup to taste

Combine all ingredients except catsup. Mix thoroughly and place in a cast-iron skillet or form into a loaf pan. Bake at 350 degrees for 1 hour. Remove from oven and cover top with catsup. Bake 30 minutes longer or until done. (*Note:* This dish can be prepared a day in advance. Keep in refrigerator both before and after cooking.)

Great for cold sandwiches!

Serves 6

R.C.'S RESTAURANT
330 East 135th Street
Kansas City, Missouri 64145
(816) 942–4999

◙ Tenderloin Tips, Korean Style

3-1/2 pounds aged beef fillet
  tips
1 cup light soy sauce
1/2 cup water
1/4 cup sesame oil
2 green onions, finely sliced
6 cloves garlic, minced
2 teaspoons sugar
2 teaspoons pear nectar
1 cup cellophane noodles
  (glass noodles)
1/2 cup cup light soy sauce
1/2 cup sesame oil
2 teaspoons olive oil
2 pounds spinach leaves,
  trimmed and washed
1/4 cup unsalted butter
1-1/2 cups carrots, cut into
  1/4-inch ovals, blanched,
  crisp
1-1/2 cups parsnips, cut into
  1/4-inch ovals, blanched,
  crisp
Salt and ground white pepper
  to taste
1 cup sliced green onion
1 teaspoon toasted sesame seed

Cube beef fillet tips. Combine soy sauce, water, sesame oil, onions, garlic, sugar, and pear nectar. Marinate beef in this mixture for 6 hours.

Boil the cellophane noodles for 2 minutes. Drain and add 1/2 cup soy sauce. Drain and keep warm. Heat 1/2 cup sesame oil in a skillet until very hot. Remove beef medallions from marinade and drain. Sauté quickly on both sides to desired doneness. In a second skillet, heat up the olive oil and sauté the spinach leaves just until wilted. Set aside. In a third pan, melt butter and heat blanched carrots and parsnips. Season with a little salt and white pepper.

Arrange cellophane noodles, meat, and vegetables attractively on a hot plate. Garnish with green onions and toasted sesame seeds. (*Note:* Rice can be substituted for the cellophane noodles.)

Serves 8

THE BRASSERIE BAR & CAFE
Westin Crown Center Hotel, One Pershing Road
Kansas City, Missouri 64108
(816) 391–4472

◙ Rich Davis's Oriental Barbecued Beef Tenderloin

1 (6-pound) whole beef
   tenderloin, trimmed
1 cup soy sauce
1/3 cup oriental toasted
   sesame oil
3 large cloves garlic, minced
1 tablespoon ground ginger
1 cup K.C. Masterpiece
   Barbecue Sauce, hickory
   flavor

Prepare a marinade by combining soy sauce, sesame oil, garlic, and ginger. Pour marinade over tenderloin in glass or enameled pan. Cover with plastic wrap and marinate overnight in refrigerator.

Remove tenderloin from marinade. Place tenderloin on a charcoal grill with moistened hickory chips added over an indirect low fire (200–225 degrees). Barbecue with lid closed, turning every 15 minutes and basting with marinade. Cook for approximately 1-1/2 hours.

For indoor barbecuing, cook in an oven preheated to 300 degrees following basting directions, to desired degree of doneness. Use a meat thermometer for best results. Serve with barbecue sauce on the side.

Serves 8

K.C. MASTERPIECE BARBECUE & GRILL
10985 Metcalf
Overland Park, Kansas 66210
(913) 345-1199

@ Tenderloin Black Forest

2 (5-pound) beef tenderloins,
    peeled and cleaned
1 (16-ounce) can dark pitted
    cherries, drained
4 large cloves garlic, pureed
1/2 cup Burgundy
1/3 cup olive oil

Combine cherries with wine, garlic, and olive oil, and let the mixture sit in refrigerator overnight.

Split tenderloins lengthwise, but not all the way through. Fill the cavity with cherry mixture and tie with butcher's twine at 2-inch intervals.

Grill meat over hot coals and cherry wood for 10 minutes on each side. Cover grill and cook for 20 more minutes. Internal temperature should reach 120 degrees for medium rare, 135 for medium.

Serves 16

EDDY'S CATERING
320 North McGee
Kansas City, Missouri 64116
(816) 842-7484

◙ Papaya Flank Steak with Diablo Sauce and Black Bean Corn Relish

1 (1-1/2–2-pound) flank steak
2 tablespoons sugar
2 tablespoons soy sauce
2 tablespoons black pepper
1 tablespoon kosher salt
1 papaya (or pineapple), sliced
  very thin (do not peel or seed
  papaya)

Sprinkle sugar, soy sauce, pepper, and salt on both sides of steak. Completely cover both sides of steak with 3/4 of the papaya slices. Press meat/fruit combination between 2 plates. Refrigerate 24 hours.

Preheat grill to medium-high heat and cook steak to desired doneness. Slice against the grain at a 45-degree angle. Serve with remaining papaya, **Diablo Sauce,** and **Black Bean Corn Relish.**

Serves 4

Diablo Sauce

4 tablespoons butter
1 tablespoon minced garlic
1 tablespoon minced shallot
1/4 cup flour
1/2 teaspoon black pepper
2 teaspoons dry mustard
1 tablespoon Heinz 57 sauce
1 (10-ounce) can beef
  consommé

Melt butter and sauté garlic and shallots. Add flour and pepper, and cook 2 minutes. Combine dry mustard, Heinz 57 sauce, and consommé, and add to mixture. Bring to a boil, then remove from heat. Serve over steak.

Makes about 1-1/2 cups

Black Bean Corn Relish

1/2 cup uncooked black beans
3 cups chicken stock
4 tablespoons butter
1 medium green pepper, diced
1 medium red pepper, diced
1 medium yellow onion, diced
1 ear fresh corn, kernels sliced
   from cob
1/2 bunch fresh cilantro,
   coarsely chopped

Cover beans with water and soak overnight. Pour off water, and boil beans in chicken stock for 20 minutes or until tender. Cool pot with beans in ice bath for quicker usage. Pour off stock. Sauté beans, peppers, corn kernels, and cilantro in butter for 3-1/2 minutes. Serve hot as an accompaniment to steak.

Serves 4

METROPOLIS AMERICAN GRILL
303 Westport Road
Kansas City, Missouri 64111
(816) 753–1550

@ Marinated Barbecued Brisket

1 (3–4-pound) beef brisket
1 (2-ounce) packet
   Stephenson's Barbeque
   Brisket Seasoning
1/3 cup plus 1 tablespoon
   Liquid Smoke
1/3 cup plus 1 tablespoon
   water

Wipe brisket with a damp cloth. Sprinkle half the packet of seasoning on both sides and edges of brisket. Dilute Liquid Smoke with water and marinate brisket in mixture overnight.

Remove meat from marinade and sprinkle remaining half packet of seasoning over entire brisket. Wrap seasoned brisket in doubled heavy aluminum foil and place fat side up in a shallow baking pan. Bake in slow oven (250 degrees) for 6 hours. Remove and slice across the grain. (*Note:* This is best made a day ahead of time.)

Serve your favorite barbecue sauce alongside this fragrant meat.

Serves 8 to 10

STEPHENSON'S OLD APPLE FARM RESTAURANT
16401 East 40 Highway
Kansas City, Missouri 64163
(816) 373-5400

◙ Smoked Pork Chop with Apple-Cranberry Relish

2 (12-ounce) pre-smoked rib
  pork chops
2 tart apples, peeled, cored,
  and chopped
1 cup fresh cranberries (use
  frozen if fresh not available)
2 tablespoons butter
1/4 cup sugar
1 cup port

Grill chops and finish in a 350-degree oven for approximately 30 minutes. While pork chops are heating, make the relish by sautéing cranberries and apples together with butter and sugar. Add wine and reduce until consistency thickens. Serve chops with relish on the side.

Serves 2

THE CAFE AT THE RITZ-CARLTON, KANSAS CITY
401 Ward Parkway
Kansas City, Missouri 64112
(816) 756–1500

◙ Pork Tenderloin with Prickly Pear Barbeque Glaze

2 pounds pork tenderloins
Salt and black pepper to taste
2 tablespoons salad oil

Trim fat and sinew from pork tenderloins, season with salt and pepper, and marinate overnight. Sear with oil in a hot skillet and roast in a medium (350-degree) oven until nearly done (about 1 hour). Brush pork with 1 cup of warm **Prickly Pear Barbeque Glaze** several times during the last 15 minutes of cooking. Slice thin and serve with a little additional glaze.

Serves 4

Prickly Pear Barbeque Glaze

2 cups catsup
2 cups prickly pear syrup*
1 cup soy sauce
1 (10-ounce) jar orange
   marmelade
1 tablespoon Tabasco
1 tablespoon chopped garlic

Combine all ingredients and bring to a slow simmer. Cook for 10 minutes, then remove from heat. Use as a finishing glaze for pork tenderloin. Refrigerate any leftover glaze to use on meats and grilled fish.

Makes about 6 cups

*Available from gourmet shops or Cahill's Desert Products (602/956–2030).

THE ROTISSERIE RESTAURANT
Doubletree Hotel at Corporate Woods, 10100 College Boulevard
Overland Park, Kansas 66210
(913) 451–6100

◙ Raspberry Mustard-Glazed Pork Roast

1 (3-1/2–4-pound) boneless pork top loin roast, tied
1-1/2 cups Flower of the Flames Raspberry Barbecue Sauce (available at gourmet shops and through Eddy's Catering)
2 tablespoons finely grated orange peel
1/4 cup fresh orange juice
1/4 cup "old style" prepared mustard
1 teaspoon minced ginger root (or 1/2 teaspoon ground ginger)
1/2 teaspoon salt
1/4 teaspoon cayenne pepper

In a small bowl, prepare glaze by combining barbecue sauce, orange peel, orange juice, mustard, ginger, salt, and cayenne pepper. Set aside.

Prepare and preheat grill to 250 degrees for indirect cooking. Place a wire rack 4 to 6 inches over drip pan, and place roast on the rack. Cover grill, opening vents slightly. Cook roast for 45 minutes and turn. Add more briquettes and apple wood chips to fire and maintain a constant temperature. Brush roast with glaze mixture every 10 minutes. Cook for another 45 minutes or until pork has a slight tinge of pink when cut a thickest part (meat thermometer should register 160 to 165 degrees).

Remove roast from grill, wrap in plastic wrap, and let stand for 10 minutes before serving.

Serves 8

EDDY'S CATERING
320 North McGee
Kansas City, Missouri 64116
(816) 842-7484

@ Hickory-Grilled Porkburger

1 pound lean ground pork
3/4 cup finely grated Italian
   bread crumbs
3/4 cup grated imported
   Romano cheese
3 cloves fresh garlic, minced
3 eggs
1/2 teaspoon salt
1/4 teaspoon black pepper
1/3 cup chopped fresh parsley
   (or 1 tablespoon dried
   flakes)
1 tablespoon chopped fresh
   basil leaf (or 2 teaspoons
   dried crushed leaf)
1 package hamburger buns
1 large red onion, sliced
1 large tomato, sliced
4–6 lettuce leaves, washed and
   dried
Marty's Bar-B-Q Sauce

Make a well in the middle of ground meat. Add bread crumbs, cheese, and spices, and mix thoroughly to distribute evenly. Separate into 4 or 5 equal parts. Moisten hands and mold meat into patties approximately 3/4- to 1-inch thick. Grill over an open flame, with moistened hickory chips added, until meat is well done (patties should not be pink in the middle). Serve on grilled hamburger buns with grilled red onions, fresh sliced tomatoes, lettuce, and barbecue sauce. (*Note:* Patties may be made up in advance and either stored in the refrigerator or frozen for up to 3 months.)

Serves 4

MARTY'S BAR-B-Q
2516 N.E. Vivion Road
Kansas City, Missouri 64118
(816) 453-2222

Sweet Endings

❖ Mihallabiyya

1 cup heavy whipping cream
4 cups milk
2 cups sugar
1 teaspoon pure vanilla extract
1/2 cup cornstarch
1 cup water
1/2 cup raisins
1/2 cup coconut
1/2 cup chopped English
  walnuts

Combine cream, milk, sugar, and vanilla in a saucepan and cook until boiling. Mix cornstarch with water and whip until smooth. Slowly add mixture to the boiled cream, constantly stirring until thickened. Remove from heat and cool slightly. Scoop into 8 serving bowls and refrigerate at least 2 hours prior to serving. Garnish with raisins, coconut, and chopped walnuts, enough to cover each little serving bowl. (*Note:* This dessert can be made in the morning and refrigerated until dinner time.)

Serves 8 to 10

CAFE NILE
8433 Wornall Road
Kansas City, Missouri 64114
(816) 361-9097

❈ White Chocolate Mousse with Raspberry Sauce

2 pounds white chocolate
10 eggs
1 cup simple syrup (1 cup
    water to 1/2 cup sugar)
3 cups heavy whipping cream
Semi-sweet chocolate shavings
    for garnish

Melt chocolate and set aside to cool. Separate eggs and set whites aside. Slowly whip simple syrup into yolks. Put mixture in double boiler over boiling water and whisk until mixture is warm to the touch. Remove and continue whipping by hand for another 2 minutes until mixture forms a "ribbon" of yolks and sugar. Slowly add melted chocolate to yolk and syrup mixture, and blend well. Continue to whip until smooth.

Whip cream until it forms soft peaks, then set aside. Whip egg whites until they form soft peaks and set aside. Fold whipped cream into the chocolate mixture first, then the whipped egg whites. Be careful not to overblend (you don't want to collapse the cream or egg whites by adding too much too fast). Chill mixture at 35 degrees for 8 hours.

Spread a pool of **Raspberry Sauce** onto dessert plates, followed by a serving of mousse. Garnish each with chocolate shavings.

Serves 8 to 10

Raspberry Sauce

10 ounces frozen raspberries,
   thawed and drained
2 tablespoons water
3 tablespoons sugar
3 tablespoons fresh lemon
   juice
2 teaspoons light rum

In a saucepan combine raspberries with water and bring to a boil over moderate heat, stirring occasionally. In a food processor fitted with the steel blade or in a blender, puree the raspberry mixture with the sugar, lemon juice, and rum. Force the puree through a fine sieve into a small bowl and cover. Let chill overnight.

Makes about 1-1/2 cups

CAFE ALLEGRO
1815 West 39th Street
Kansas City, Missouri 64105
(816) 561-3663

❈ Sweet Potato Pie
with Cinnamon Ice Cream

1/8 cup all-purpose flour
1/4 teaspoon ground cinnamon
1/4 teaspoon ground nutmeg
1/4 teaspoon ground ginger
1/4 teaspoon finely ground
  cloves
1/4 teaspoon salt
1 cup brown sugar
3 eggs
1 (1-pound) can sweet potatoes
1/4 cup corn syrup
1-1/2 cups milk
1 (9-inch) prepared pie crust

Sift together flour and spices into a large bowl. Add brown sugar and mix until smooth. Add eggs one at a time, mixing well after each addition. Whip sweet potatoes until smooth, then add egg mixture. Slowly add corn syrup and milk, mixing gently until smooth. Bake at 350 degrees on middle rack of oven for 30 to 40 minutes. Serve warm and top with Cinnamon Ice Cream.

Serves 8

Cinnamon Ice Cream

1 quart heavy whipping cream
12 egg yolks
1 cup sugar
2 tablespoons ground
  cinnamon
1 teaspoon vanilla extract

Combine all ingredients and blend well. Pour into a saucepan and heat slowly, stirring constantly just until liquid begins to boil. Refrigerate for 3 to 4 hours or overnight. Churn as directed in an ice cream maker. Freeze until desired consistency.

Makes 1 quart

THE CAFE AT THE RITZ-CARLTON, KANSAS CITY
401 Ward Parkway
Kansas City, Missouri 64112
(816) 756–1500

✤ Savoy's Irish Whiskey Pie

3 tablespoons water
6 tablespoons Irish whiskey
4 egg yolks
2/3 cup sugar
1-1/2 cups heavy cream
1 scant tablespoon unflavored
   gelatine
1 graham cracker pie shell
Bittersweet chocolate shavings
   for garnish

Combine water and Irish whiskey. Blend egg yolks, sugar, and 3 tablespoons of whiskey/water mixture in a bowl. Place remaining whiskey/water mixture on the stove to warm. Whip heavy cream until stiff and add to egg yolk mixture; gently cut cream into mixture. Remove whiskey/water mixture from stove and add gelatin. Dissolve until no lumps remain and sauce is smooth. Cool gelatin sauce and blend into egg yolk mixture. Pour mixture into graham cracker pie shell. Garnish with chocolate shavings.

Serves 6–8

SAVOY GRILL
9th and Central Streets
Kansas City, Missouri 64105
(816) 842–3890

❉ Lemon Almond Tart

2 cups pastry flour
4 tablespoons sugar
1 stick unsalted butter, chilled
1 whole egg
1 egg yolk
Pinch of salt
2 cups uncooked rice or beans
Powdered sugar

Sift flour and sugar into food processor outfitted with steel blade. Add butter and process until no lumps remain. In a separate bowl, beat egg and egg yolk with salt until salt is dissolved. Add egg mixture to flour mixture and stir gently until egg is completely absorbed. Wrap in plastic wrap and place in refrigerator for at least 4 hours.

Line a 10-inch tart pan with dough, then cover dough with baking paper or foil and fill with rice or beans (this holds dough down and keeps it from rising.). Prebake for 10 to 12 minutes at 350 degrees or until lightly browned. Remove paper or foil and fill with rice or beans. Remove paper or foil with rice or beans and set aside to cool. Fill with **Lemon Almond Tart Filling**. Finish baking at 350 degrees until golden brown and set (about 25 to 30 minutes). Allow to cool and dust with powdered sugar. Serve at room temperature.

Serves 8 to 10

Lemon Almond Tart Filling

1-1/4 cups sugar
Zest of 3 lemons
1/4 cup sliced and blanched
   almonds
4 whole eggs
1 stick unsalted butter,
   softened
Juice of 4 lemons

In a food processor, combine sugar, lemon zest, and almonds until very finely chopped. Add eggs one by one with motor running, then add butter in little pieces. Add lemon juice in a slow stream until blended.

Makes about 3 cups

JOE D'S WINE BAR & CAFE
6227 Brookside Plaza
Kansas City, Missouri 64113
(816) 333–6116

❖ Chocolate Peanut Butter Ice Cream Pie

15 chocolate sandwich cookies
1/2 cup dry-roasted peanuts
Vegetable cooking spray
4 tablespoons butter or
  margarine, melted
3 quarts chocolate ice cream
7 (1.8-ounce) chocolate-
  covered peanut butter cups
1 cup heavy whipping cream
2 tablespoons sugar
1 (8-ounce) jar milk chocolate
  fudge topping
1/4 cup strong coffee
2 tablespoons coffee-flavored
  liqueur

Preheat oven to 400 degrees. In food processor with metal blade attached, blend chocolate sandwich cookies and peanuts until finely chopped. Spray a 9-inch pie plate with cooking spray. Set aside 1 tablespoon cookie mixture for garnish.

In pie plate, mix together butter and remaining cookie mixture by hand. Press mixture onto bottom and up sides of pie plate. Bake 8 minutes. Cool on wire rack.

Take ice cream out of freezer and place in refrigerator about 40 minutes to soften slightly. Coarsely chop peanut butter cups. In a bowl, use a spoon to mix softened ice cream with chopped peanut butter cups. Spoon into cooled cookie crust. Freeze until firm (overnight).

Beat heavy whipping cream and sugar until stiff peaks form. Spoon whipped cream into decorating bag; pipe rosettes on outside edge of pie and on top. Sprinkle 1 tablespoon reserved cookie crumb mixture on top of pie. Place pie in freezer, but do not cover until whipped cream has hardened.

To serve, let pie stand at room temperature 15 minutes for easier slicing. In a 1-quart saucepan over low heat, heat fudge topping until hot; stir in coffee and coffee liqueur until blended. Serve with warm fudge sauce.

Serves 8 to 12

K.C. MASTERPIECE BARBECUE & GRILL
10985 Metcalf
Overland Park, Kansas 66210
(913) 345–1199

✺ Arizona Chocolate Pecan Pie

3 ounces unsweetened
  chocolate
3 tablespoons unsalted butter
5 eggs
1 cup brown sugar
1-1/2 cups dark Karo corn
  syrup
1-1/2 teaspoons vanilla
2 tablespoons rum
2-1/4 cups chopped pecans
1/2 pint whipping cream

Melt chocolate and butter, then cool slightly. Beat eggs lightly, then cream in sugar and corn syrup. Mix in vanilla, rum, and pecans, and pour into unbaked **Acadian Pie Pastry** shell. Bake at 400 degrees for 10 minutes, then at 350 degrees until set (about 50 minutes) or until toothpick comes out clean. Allow to set before slicing. Best if served warm, topped with a dollup of slightly whipped cream.

Serves 8

Acadian Pie Pastry

5-1/2 cups flour
1 pound lard
1 teaspoon salt
1 teaspoon vinegar
1 egg
Water (up to 1 cup)

Cut lard into flour and salt. Add remaining ingredients and mix until just moist. Cut in thirds. Roll out to fill three 10-inch pie pans. (*Note:* Crust can be prepared in advance, tightly wrapped, and chilled.) Use 1 crust for **Arizona Pecan Pie** and freeze the other 2 for future use.

Makes 3 pie shells

THE ROTISSERIE RESTAURANT
Doubletree Hotel at Corporate Woods, 10100 College Boulevard
Overland Park, Kansas 66210
(913) 451-6100

❋ Chocolate Truffle Cake

16 ounces semi-sweet
  chocolate
1 stick unsalted butter
1-1/2 teaspoons all-purpose
  flour
1-1/2 teaspoons sugar
1 teaspoon hot water
4 eggs, beaten

Melt chocolate and butter together in a double boiler. Add flour, sugar, and water, blending well. Add beaten eggs to mixture very slowly, blending well. Turn into a greased 8-inch springform pan. Bake for exactly 15 minutes at 425 degrees. Cool completely. (Center will sink and crack.) Cover with **Whipped Topping**.

Serves 8

Whipped Topping

1 cup heavy unsweetened
  cream, whipped
Chocolate shavings, as needed

Spread top of finished cake with a thick layer of whipped cream. Decorate sides with small rosettes of whipped cream. Mark off 8 portions and place a rosette on top of each portion. Sprinkle chocolate shavings over top.

Makes 2 cups

FEDORA CAFE & BAR
210 West 47th Street
Kansas City, Missouri 64112
(816) 561–6565

❖ Delicious Carrot Cake

1-1/4 cups oil
1 cup brown sugar, packed
1 cup sugar
4 eggs
1 cup flour
1 cup whole wheat flour
1 teaspoon salt
2 teaspoons baking soda
2 teaspoons baking powder
2 teaspoons ground cinnamon
3 cups finely shredded carrots
8-1/2 ounces crushed
 pineapple, drained
1/2 cup finely chopped
 walnuts

In a large bowl blend together oil and sugars. Add eggs one at a time, beating until blended. In another bowl sift together both flours, salt, soda, baking powder, and cinnamon. Add the flour mixture about 1/3 at a time to the oil mixture, beating just enough to blend.

Fold carrots, then pineapple and nuts, into the batter. Pour batter into 2 greased and lightly floured 9-inch round cake pans. Bake in a preheated 350-degree oven for 35 to 40 minutes or until a toothpick inserted in the center of each comes out clean. Cool the cakes in the pans on a rack for 10 minutes. Turn cakes out on the rack and cool completely.

Layer the cake with **Coconut-Pecan Frosting** and spread sides and top with **Lemon Cream Cheese Frosting.** (*Note:* Prepare a day in advance. Unfrosted cakes may be wrapped in airtight plastic wrap and refrigerated for 5 to 6 days or frozen for 2 to 3 months. If frosted, the cakes may be stored in refrigerator for a week or more.)

Serves 8

Coconut-Pecan Frosting

1 cup evaporated milk
1 cup sugar   •
3 egg yolks
1/2 cup butter
1 teaspoon vanilla extract
1 (3-1/2 ounce) can flaked
 coconut
1 cup chopped pecans

Combine milk, sugar, egg yolks, butter, and vanilla in a saucepan. Cook over medium heat, stirring constantly, until mixture thickens. Add flaked coconut and pecans. Beat until cool. Make sure frosting is of a spreading consistency.

Lemon Cream Cheese Frosting

1 (8-ounce) package cream
   cheese, softened
1/4 cup butter, softened
2 cups powdered sugar
1-1/2 teaspoons vanilla extract
1 tablespoon grated lemon rind

In a large mixing bowl, mash cream cheese, add butter, and then cream together until well mixed and fluffy. Add sugar (sift first if lumpy) to mixture and beat until well blended. Blend in vanilla and lemon rind. (*Note:* This will keep in the refrigerator for about 1 week.)

ALL WRAPPED UP

▦ Frangelico Cheesecake

1 (9-inch) prepared cheesecake
8 tablespoons chopped toasted
   filberts

Slice cheesecake into 8 portions. Spoon
4 tablespoons **Frangelico Sauce** over each
piece. Top slices with 1 tablespoon toasted
filberts.

Serves 8

Frangelico Sauce

1 cup light corn syrup
1/2 pound butter
1/4 cup Frangelico liqueur

In a saucepan bring corn syrup to boil.
Cut butter into pieces. Add to corn syrup
while stirring constantly. Remove from
heat and chill until well cooled. When cool,
stir in liqueur. Bring to room temperature
before serving.

Makes 2 cups

FIGLIO
209 West 46th Terrace
Kansas City, Missouri 64112
(816) 561–0505

❀ Fresh Fruit and Sour Cream

1/2 pint raspberries
1/2 pint blackberries
1/2 pint strawberries, cut into
   1/4-inch pieces
1/2 pint blueberries
2 tablespoons brown sugar
1 tablespoon Triple Sec
1-1/2 cups sour cream
6 fresh mint leaves

Wash fruit and place in a large mixing bowl. In a small mixing bowl dissolve brown sugar in Triple Sec. Add sour cream. Whip until evenly mixed. Add to berries and fold all together. Serve in large wine glasses, and top each with a mint leaf.

Serves 6

FITZPATRICK'S

❋ Fresh Berry Trifle with Anglaise Sauce

24 ladyfingers
1/2 cup Grand Marnier
1/2 cup black cherry jam
1 cup fresh berries
    (strawberries, raspberries,
    or blueberries)
1 cup heavy cream, whipped

Into the bottom of 4 wine glasses pour 1 tablespoon of **Anglaise Sauce.** Place three ladyfingers soaked with 1 tablespoon of Grand Marnier into each glass. Spread top of sponge with 1 tablespoon of jam. Place 1 tablespoon of berries on top of jam, followed by 1 tablespoon of **Anglaise Sauce** and 1 tablespoon of whipped cream. Repeat process a second time. Top each trifle with a rosette of whipped cream and a fresh berry.

Serves 4

Anglaise Sauce

2/3 cup half-and-half
2/3 cup heavy cream
1/3 cup granulated sugar
3/4 teaspoon cornstarch
3 egg yolks
1 teaspoon vanilla extract

In the top section of a double boiler, place half-and-half and heavy cream over simmering water. Allow cream to heat until steaming, stirring often. In a mixing bowl, thoroughly combine sugar and cornstarch. Add yolks and vanilla, beating in well to make a thick paste. Add paste to steaming cream in double boiler, whipping constantly. Continue to cook sauce in double boiler until thick and shiny. Remove when thickened. Strain and cool completely.

Makes 2 cups

PLAZA III–THE STEAKHOUSE
4749 Pennsylvania
Kansas City, Missouri 64112
(816) 753–0000

▦ Melon Gastrique

1 firm cantaloupe (slightly
   underripe)
1/2 pound sugar
1/2 quart lemon juice
1 tablespoon honey
Lime wedges

Combine all ingredients in a saucepan and cook 5 minutes; let cool. Slice melon and arrange in a shallow pan. Pour syrup over melon slices and marinate for 2 hours. To serve, fan melon slices across a plate and then pour marinade over all. Serve with lime wedges.

Serves 4

LA MEDITERRANÉE
9058-B Metcalf Avenue
Overland Park, Kansas 66212
(913) 341-9595

Italian Cannoli

2 cups flour
2 tablespoons sugar
1/8 teaspoon salt
1/2 cup lard
1/2 cup strong coffee
1 slightly beaten egg white mixed with 1 tablespoon water
Oil for deep frying
36 standard cannoli tubes (found at gourmet groceries or cooking stores)
Powdered sugar
36 maraschino cherries, sliced in half

Combine flour, sugar, and salt. Work lard into mixture until crumbly. Add coffee. Mix dough well and roll until thin as a dime (if available, use flat roller on home pasta machine). Cut a 3-1/2 inch circle. Wrap dough around a cannoli tube and seal with beaten egg white. Fry in deep fat until golden brown. Remove with long-handled fork and let drain well on absorbent paper towels. Repeat the process until all dough is used. (*Note:* Shells may be stored for 2 to 4 weeks.)

When ready to serve, stuff with **Cannoli Filling** and top with plenty of powdered sugar. Place half a maraschino cherry on each end and serve immediately.

Makes 3 dozen

Cannoli Filling

3 pounds ricotta cheese, well drained
1-1/2 cups powdered sugar
1-1/2 tablespoons grated orange peel (optional)
1-1/2 teaspoons vanilla
3/4 cup finely chopped Hershey bar with almonds
1/4 teaspoon cinnamon
1-1/2 tablespoons minced maraschino cherries

Beat ricotta cheese, adding powdered sugar gradually until smooth. Add orange peel, vanilla, Hershey bar, cinnamon, and cherries. Mix well and refrigerate overnight.

CASCONE'S ITALIAN RESTAURANT
3733 North Oak Trafficway
Kansas City, Missouri 64116
(816) 454-7977

❇ Baklava

2-1/2 pounds walnut meats,
    coarsley ground
1 tablespoon cinnamon
1-1/2 cups sugar
1-1/2 pounds butter, melted
2 pounds phyllo pastry

Mix walnuts with cinnamon and sugar. Grease a 10-inch by 15-inch pan with some of the melted butter. Place 6 phyllo sheets in pan, brushing each generously with melted butter. Sprinkle with a thin layer of nuts and then cover with 3 phyllo sheets, brushing each with melted butter. Alternate in this way until walnuts and phyllo are all used, topping finally with 6 buttered phyllo sheets. Cut pastry into small diamond shapes. Bake in a 300-degree oven for 1-1/2 hours until lightly browned. Remove from oven and pour cool **Baklava Syrup** over hot pastry.

Makes 75 small servings

Baklava Syrup

3 cups sugar
2 cups water
1 lemon rind
1 stick cinnamon
3 cloves
Juice of 1/2 lemon
1/2 cup honey

Bring sugar, water, lemon rind, cinnamon, and cloves to a boil. Lower heat and simmer 10 minutes. Remove lemon rind, cinnamon stick, and cloves. Add lemon juice and honey; bring to a slow boil. Cool.

Makes 5-1/2 cups

VETTA'S GRECIAN CUISINE

Restaurants

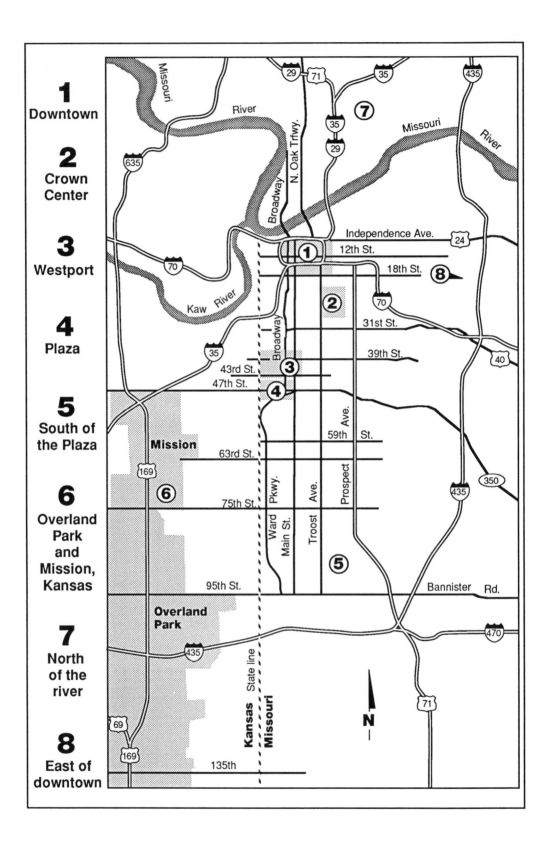

≋ Restaurant Listings

The following listings offer additional information about the restaurants represented in the recipe sections of this book.

KEY:
Prices/credit cards: $ (under $10); $$ ($10 to $20); $$$ ($20 and up); □ (credit cards accepted); no □ (credit cards not accepted)
Dress: C (casual); D (dressy)
Map Location: (1) Downtown; (2) Crown Center; (3) Westport; (4) Country Club Plaza; (5) South of the Plaza; (6) Shawnee Mission, Kansas; (7) North of the river; (8) East of downtown

All Wrapped Up. (*Editor's note:* Homemade casseroles, soups, and desserts delighted diners at this Victorian home restaurant. Although closed now, we are pleased to share a sampling of the recipes.)

The American Restaurant, 200 E. 25th St., atop Hall's Crown Center, Kansas City, MO 64108; (816) 426-1133. A haven of quiet elegance, the American Restaurant boasts superior cuisine, fine wine, and a wonderful view of the city. The American regional fare features unusual vegetables, game, seafood, steak, and veal. $$$; □; D; (2)

Ande-lei's Cafe. (*Editor's note:* Although this restaurant has closed its doors, the authentic Venezuelan dishes are still stand-outs.)

The Bistro at The Classic Cup, 4130 Pennsylvania, Kansas City, MO 64111; (816) 756-0771. The Bistro is noted for its contemporary American Heartland cuisine, fresh seasonal products, and bustling, friendly atmosphere. $$; □; C; (3)

The Brasserie Bar & Cafe, Westin Crown Center Hotel, One Pershing Rd., Kansas City, MO 64108; (816) 391-4472. International cuisine and daily heart-healthy meals approved by the AMA are offered in pleasant and relaxing surroundings. $; □; C; (2)

Cafe Allegro, 1815 W. 39th St., Kansas City, MO 64111; (816) 561-3663. This New York–style restaurant offers a variety of contemporary seasonal cuisine that includes an eclectic array of fresh fish, veal, game and pasta. $$–$$$; □; C; (3)

The Cafe at the Ritz-Carlton, Kansas City, 401 Ward Pkwy., Kansas City, MO 64112; (816) 756-1500. This elegant hotel restaurant provides the best of American cuisine in an ambiance of warmth and elegance, enhanced by crystal chandeliers, fine art, and fresh flowers. $$; ☐; D; (4)

Cafe Nile, 8433 Wornall Rd., Kansas City, MO 64114; (816) 361-9097. Noted for its appetizing Mediterranean cuisine, this small Waldo bistro draws raves for its seafood bisque, rack of lamb, Shrimp Garlic, and Beef Oscar dishes. $$; ☐; C; (5)

Californos, 4124 Pennsylvania, Kansas City, MO 64111; (816) 531-7878. The congenial setting and helpful service make lunch or dinner here a treat. Innovative eclectic cuisine and fresh fish grilled to order are what this place does best. $$; ☐; C; (3)

Cascone's Italian Restaurant & Lounge, 323 Armour Rd., N. Kansas City, MO 64116; (816) 471-4400. There's plenty of baseball memorabilia here along with half-pound hamburgers, London broil, prime rib, and terrific tenderloins. $; ☐; C; (7)

The Classic Cup (Plaza), 310 W. 47th St., Kansas City, MO 64112; (816) 753-1009. This bright, cheery cafe on the Country Club Plaza features fresh, seasonal menu items. In warm weather the outdoor patio offers limited menu service. $$; ☐; C; (4)

The Coffee Shop, Kansas City Marriott Downtown, 200 W. 12th St., Kansas City, MO 64105; (816) 421-6800. This downtown restaurant is a nice oasis from the hustle of the Bartle Hall convention center. It features good menu choices at reasonable prices. If you're in a hurry, the fast-paced "a la carte" service is helpful. $; ☐; C; (1)

Coyote Grill, 4843 Johnson Dr., Mission, KS 66205; (913) 362-3333. A Southwestern theme highlights a delightful menu that features innovative pasta, seafood, beef, and chicken dishes. The atmosphere is as much fun as the food. $–$$; ☐; C; (6)

E.B.T Restaurant, 1310 Carondelet Dr., Kansas City, MO 64114; (816) 942-8870. Residents and out-of-towners come here to sample the American and French-style cuisine served in a formal, elegant atmosphere. $$; ☐; D; (5)

Eddy's Catering, 320 N. McGee, Kansas City, MO 64116; (816) 842-7484. Eddy's Catering has been serving the people of Kansas City and their guests for over 60 years. Eddy's specializes in catering for corporate and social events. For the more casual events, Eddy's offers chicken from their Popeye's franchise. $$–$$$; ☐

Fedora Cafe & Bar, 210 W. 47th St., Kansas City, MO 64112; (816) 561-6565. A European-style bistro, Fedora keeps up with culinary trends, offering a variety of international dishes in a polished, upscale environment. Orechiette with Grilled Chicken and Smoked Corn and Goat Cheese Quesadilla are house favorites. $$–$$$; □; D; (4)

Figlio, 209 W. 46th Terr., Kansas City, MO 64112; (816) 561-0505. Friendly surroundings and fresh pasta make this Italian restaurant on the Country Club Plaza a favorite after-shop stop of residents and tourists alike. $$; □; C; (4)

Fitzpatrick's. (*Editor's note:* Though no longer in business, this restaurant offered dishes that were tasty and upscale. We are pleased to retain a sample here.)

Jasper's Italian Restaurant, 405 W. 75th St., Kansas City, MO 64114; (816) 363-3003. Offering traditional tableside service, this Mobil Four-Star and Travel/Holiday Award–winning restaurant is famous for its superior Northern Italian cuisine such as Scampi Livornese and Lobster Ravioli Argosta. $$$; □; D; (5)

Joe D's Wine Bar & Cafe, 6227 Brookside Plaza, Kansas City, MO 64113; (816) 333-6116. This neighborhood watering hole has become one of Brookside's busiest hangouts. Blessed with an abundant wine list, Joe D's also features excellent eclectic cuisine at reasonable prices. $$; □; C; (5)

Johnny Cascone's Italian Restaurant, 6863 W. 91st St.,Overland Park, KS 66212; (913) 381-6837. Like its counterpart in North Kansas City, this establishment serves Northern and Southern Italian dishes in a friendly, comfortable atmosphere highlighted by a variety of pasta, sausage, and veal specialties. $$; □; C; (6)

K.C. Masterpiece Barbecue & Grill, 10985 Metcalf, Overland Park, KS 66210, (913) 345-1199; 4747 Wyandotte St., Kansas City, MO 64112, (816) 531-3332. A combination of Kansas City–style barbecue, Western grilling, and Southern cooking techniques make this restaurant unique. Top off baby back ribs or smoked pork tenderloin with luscious Chocolate Peanut Butter Ice Cream Pie. $$; □; C; (6)

Kiki's Bon Ton Maison, 1515 Westport Rd., Kansas City, MO 64111; (816) 931-9417. Serving kicky Cajun/Creole dishes, Kiki's offers delights such as crab cakes and gumbo with a distinctly New Orleans–style flair. $, □; C; (3)

La Mediterranée, 9058-B Metcalf Ave., Overland Park, KS 66212; (913) 341-9595. Classic French dishes served in elegant surroundings makes this former Country Club Plaza restaurant a long-time favorite with Kansas Citians. Lunch is one of the best buys in town. $$–$$$; □; D; (4)

La Scalla Italian Restaurant. (*Editor's note:* This former Kansas City restaurant specialized in Italian and American fare, and the recipes offered here attest to the popularity it enjoyed.)

Mama Stuffeati's Ristorante. (*Editor's note:* This popular Westport eatery was a favorite to many, and it's a pleasure to retain a taste of the former menu.)

Marty's Bar-B-Q, 2516 N.E. Vivion Rd., Kansas City, MO 64118; (816) 453-2222. This neighborhood place serves up barbecue specialties such as ribs, Italian sausage, beef, pork, ham, and chicken in a friendly, family-oriented atmosphere. Be sure to try the Smoked Chicken Lemonada, Italian-style barbecue. $; ☐; C; (7)

Metropolis American Grill, 303 Westport Rd., Kansas City, MO 64111; (816) 753-1550. The contemporary, high-tech setting and innovative cuisine make this New York–style establishment a Kansas City favorite. Dishes are always colorful and offer a variety of cross-cultural items. $$; ☐; C; (3)

Michael Forbes Grill, 7539 Wornall Rd., Kansas City, MO 64114; (816) 444-5445. This neighborhood hangout draws people from around the city who come to soak in the congenial atmosphere, good food, and drinks. Main entrees feature a variety of steaks, seafood, and chicken dishes. $–$$; ☐; C; (5)

Milano, 2450 Grand Ave., Crown Center, Kansas City, MO 64108; (816) 426-1130. Northern Italian food is the specialty here, with offerings like chicken tenderloin, veal, bow-tie pasta, and pizza, served in the soothing surroundings of an enclosed glass pavilion. $$; ☐; C; (2)

Paradise Diner, 11327 W. 95th St., Overland Park, KS 66214; (913) 894-2222. Trendy and chic with tile floors and bright lights, the Paradise Diner is a bustling, fun place that serves everything from salads and burgers to innovative Southwestern cuisine. $–$$; ☐; C; (6)

Parkway 600 Grill, 600 Ward Pkwy., Kansas City, MO 64112; (816) 931-6600. The convivial indoor setting and summer courtyard provide a respite from shopping on the Country Club Plaza. Time-tested favorites include farm-fresh catfish, chicken and dumplings, plus steak and seafood. $$; ☐; C; (4)

The Peppercorn Duck Club, Hyatt Regency Crown Center, 2345 McGee St., Kansas City, MO 64108; (816) 421-1234. Elegant without being stuffy, the Peppercorn Duck Club features roast duck as the main attraction, followed by beef, veal, and lamb dishes, and the deliciously decadent Ultra Chocolatta Bar for dessert. $$$; ☐; D; (2)

Plaza III–The Steakhouse, 4749 Pennsylvania, Kansas City, MO 64112; (816) 753-0000. This traditional formal steak house offers steaks in all sizes, including a thundering 32-ounce Kansas City strip, as well as daintier portions of beef, seafood, chicken, and ribs. $$–$$$; □; D; (4)

Raphael Restaurant, The Raphael Hotel, 325 Ward Pkwy., Kansas City, MO 64112; (816) 756-3800. Cozy seating and traditional continental cuisine served with a contemporary American flair are part of the charm of this intimate hotel restaurant on the Country Club Plaza. $$; □; C; (4)

R.C.'s Restaurant & Lounge, 330 E. 135th St., Kansas City, MO 64145; (816) 942-4999. Finger-lickin' good pan-fried chicken served family style are why people come from around the city to dine at R.C.'s. An over-60 and under-12 menu is offered. $$; □; C; (5)

Remington's, Adam's Mark Hotel, 9103 E. 39th St., Kansas City, MO 64133; (816) 737-4733. This Western-influenced restaurant features an impressive collection of Western art along with steaks, game, and grilled seafood (there's buffalo, rattlesnake, and alligator for unusual tastes). $$; □; C; (8)

The Rotisserie Restaurant, Doubletree Hotel at Corporate Woods, 10100 College Blvd., Overland Park, KS 66210; (913) 451-6100. American dining with a touch of continental and Southwestern accents presents an interesting mix here. Dishes feature dry aged beef, prime rib, seafood, and chicken. $$; □; C; (8)

The Savoy Grill, 9th and Central Sts., Kansas City, MO 64105; (816) 842-3890. A vintage gem tucked away in the depths of downtown, the venerable Savoy Grill is famous for its seafood and beef. Offerings include Lobster Thermidor and the kind of prime steak for which Kansas City is famous. $$$; □; C; (1)

Stephenson's Apple Tree Inn Restaurant, 5755 N.W. Northwood Rd., Kansas City, MO 64151; (816) 587-9300. Hickory-smoked beef, ham, and chicken from recipes that are family traditions, fresh fruit daiquiris, and wholesome prices make this restaurant worth the drive. $$; □; C; (7)

Stephenson's Old Apple Farm Restaurant, 16401 E. 40 Hwy., Kansas City, MO 64163; (816) 373-5400. Along with fresh apple cider, apple dumplings, and apple fritters, this charming rustic restaurant serves up some of the best hickory-smoked chicken and ribs in town. $$; □; C; (8)

Trattoria Marco Polo, 7512 Wornall Rd., Kansas City, MO 64114; (816) 361-0900. Made-from-scratch sauces and fresh pasta have brought raves for this bustling Waldo bistro's Northern and Southern Italian cuisine. Charcoal-grilled steaks, seafood, veal, and homemade cannoli ice cream round out the fare. $; □; C; (5)

Vetta's Grecian Cuisine. (*Editor's note:* Though no longer in operation, we are pleased to share some of the excellent Greek dishes that diners once enjoyed at Vetta's.)

West Side Cafe, 723 Southwest Blvd., Kansas City, MO 64108; (816) 472-0010. This tiny-but-terrific place features excellent Middle-Eastern cuisine served in informal surroundings. If they have it, ask for chutney with your meal. $$; no □; C; (1)

◼ Restaurant Index

▤ Recipe Index

The bold asterisk (*) preceding a recipe title indicates a "recipe within a recipe"; that is, one that appears within the preparation instructions for a primary recipe, but which in some cases could stand alone or be served with another favorite dish.

BEGINNINGS

Salmon Ceviche, 29
Shredded Romaine Salad, 4
Southwest Flyers, 31
    *Chili Honey Sauce, 31
Springtime Lamb Salad with Walnut Vinaigrette, 10
    *Walnut Vinaigrette, 11
Stephenson's Potato Soup, 14
Vegetarian Minestrone, 19
Wild Rice Soup, 16

MAIN COURSES

Baked Chicken 'n' Butter and Cream, 65
Bon Ton Poulet, 70
Breast of Chicken Oskar, 66
    *Holland Rusks, 66
    *Béarnaise Sauce, 67
Breast of Chicken with Corn Bread Date Stuffing and Madeira Wine Sauce, 69
    *Madeira Wine Sauce, 69
Chicken and Cheese Pasta, 48
Chicken Broccoli Skillet, 68
Chicken Cacciatore Savina Marie, 60
Chicken Georgina, 61
    *Beer Cheese Sauce, 61
Chicken Sicilian, 62
Duck Provençale, 72
Egyptian Salmon, 56
Golden Potato-Crusted Snapper with Braised Wild Mushrooms and
    Red Pepper Vinaigrette, 52
    *Red Pepper Vinaigrette, 53
Grilled Chicken with Mango-Avocado Salsa, 64
    *Mango-Avocado Salsa, 64
Grilled Sea Scallops with Pancetta, 50
    *Aioli Sauce, 50
Grilled Tuna Niçoise with Balsamic Vinaigrette, 59
    *Balsamic Vinaigrette, 59
Halibut Fillet with Red Pepper Beurre Blanc, 51
    *Beurre Blanc, 51
Hickory-Grilled Porkburger, 90
Lime-Grilled Breast of Chicken, 63
Linguine Con Salmone, 45
Marinated Barbecued Brisket, 86

Papaya Flank Steak with Diablo Sauce and Black Bean Corn Relish, 84
    *Diablo Sauce, 84
    *Black Bean Corn Relish, 85
Parmesan-Crusted Veal Chop, 78
Pasta with Vodka Sauce and Sun-Dried Tomatoes, 44
Pepper Tuna, 58
Pescado Yucateco, 54
    *Olive and Red Pepper Sauce, 54
Pheasant Madeira, 71
Pork Tenderloin with Prickly Pear Barbeque Glaze, 88
    *Prickly Pear Barbeque Glaze, 88
Rack of Lamb with Raspberry Mint Sauce, 73
Raspberry Mustard-Glazed Pork Roast, 89
R.C.'s Skillet Meat Loaf, 80
Rich Davis's Oriental Barbecued Beef Tenderloin, 82
Salmon in Parchment, 55
    *Herb Butter, 55
Salmon with Hazelnut Lime Butter, 57
    *Hazelnut Lime Butter, 57
Seafood Sauté and Pasta, 47
Shrimp Coconut, 49
Smoked Pork Chop with Apple-Cranberry Relish, 87
Smoked Salmon Pasta, 46
Spaghetti Squash Alfredo, 42
Spaghettini Napoletana, 43
Spanokotyropeta, 41
Stuffed Veal Cutlets aux Quatre Fromages, 74
    *Basil Camembert Butter, 75
Tenderloin Black Forest, 83
Tenderloin Tips, Korean Style, 81
Veal Lemonada, 79
    *Butter and White Wine Sauce, 79
Veal Lemonata, 77
Veal Scallopini and Peppers, 76

SWEET ENDINGS

Arizona Chocolate Pecan Pie, 100
    *Acadian Pie Pastry, 100
Baklava, 109
    *Baklava Syrup, 109
Chocolate Peanut Butter Ice Cream Pie, 99
Chocolate Truffle Cake, 101
    *Whipped Topping, 101

▨ About the Authors

With nearly 20 books to her credit, author and publisher Shifra Stein is the creator of the acclaimed *Day Trips* series for Kansas City and other major metropolitan areas. She has authored numerous guides to Kansas City, among them *A Kid's Guide to Kansas City.* She has also co-authored *The All-American Barbecue Book* and *All About Barbecue: Kansas City-Style.* An award-winning food and travel journalist, Ms. Stein is the former restaurant critic for the *Kansas City Star,* and for years she hosted a syndicated food and travel segment aired nationally on 150 stations on the WAXWORKS Radio Network.

Ms. Stein is a member of the Society of American Travel Writers and recently received a Fellowship from the University of Missouri Kansas City's Greater Kansas City Writing Project. She currently offers life-changing journaling workshops and leads journaling seminars in conjunction with area counseling organizations, schools, and churches. A well-known speaker, Ms. Stein also provides a variety of presentations for groups, including "Day Trips," "Great Romantic Getaways," and "Travel Safety on the Road." For more information on Shifra Stein Seminars, call (913) 262-9456.

Karen Adler started a publishing firm, Pig Out Publications, in 1988, launching a line of successful barbecue cookbooks that includes *The Passion of Barbeque, Barbecue Greats Memphis Style, Texas Barbecue,* and *Hooked on Fish on the Grill,* which she also authored. Her background in book marketing and promotion played a key role in the success of *Beyond Parsley* and *Above & Beyond Parsley,* the nationally acclaimed cookbooks published by the Junior League of Kansas City, Missouri. Most recently, she and Jane Doyle Guthrie co-authored *A Kansas City Christmas Cookbook.* Several of Ms. Adler's company's books have received awards from the Mid America Publishers Association, including Best Regional Book for *Texas Barbecue,* Honorable Mention Best Regional Book for *Day Trips From San Antonio and Austin,* and Best Total Sales for *Day Trips From Nashville.*

An accomplished gourmet cook, Ms. Adler has appeared often in televised cooking demonstrations on area stations. She is a founding member of the Kansas City Chapter of the American Institute of Wine and Food and a member of the International Association of Culinary Professionals, The James Beard Foundation, and the National Barbeque Asssociation.

Both authors make their home in Kansas City and are currently at work on local and regional cookbooks and travel guides.

Order Form

ORDER DIRECT—CALL (800) 877-3119 OR FAX (816) 531-6113

Please rush the following book(s) to me:

_____ copy(s) **DALLAS CUISINE** for $14.95
_____ copy(s) **SAN DIEGO CUISINE** for $12.95
_____ copy(s) **NASHVILLE CUISINE** for $12.95
_____ copy(s) **MEMPHIS CUISINE** for $12.95
_____ copy(s) **KANSAS CITY CUISINE** for $14.95
_____ copy(s) **SAN ANTONIO CUISINE** for $14.95
_____ copy(s) **A KANSAS CITY CHRISTMAS COOKBOOK** for $14.95
_____ copy(s) **PURE PRAIRIE** for $15.95
_____ copy(s) **DAY TRIPS FROM NASHVILLE** for $9.95
_____ copy(s) **DAY TRIPS FROM KANSAS CITY** for $10.95
_____ copy(s) **DAY TRIPS FROM SAN ANTONIO AND AUSTIN** for $11.95

Shipping and handling to be added as follows:
    1 book = $3.75
    2 books = $4.75
    3–5 books = $6.00

METHOD OF PAYMENT

_____ Enclosed is my check for $_____ (payable to Two Lane Press, Inc.)
_____ Please charge to my credit card: ____VISA ____ MasterCard

Acct.#_____

Signature _____

SHIP TO:_____ GIFT/SHIP TO: _____

_____   _____
_____   _____
_____   _____
_____   _____

MAIL COMPLETED ORDER FORM TO:

Two Lane Press, Inc. ✺ 4245 Walnut Street ✺ Kansas City, MO 64111